{An} Unsinkable Soul

{An} Unsinkable Soul

22 *Inspiring Bounceback Stories and Reasons to Keep Going*

First Edition Anthology

Advance Praise for {An} Unsinkable Soul

I would like to thank you for writing *{An} Unsinkable Soul*. The authors in this book have enlightened upon many areas of life that people around the world are facing in their daily lives. Reading this book has opened up an internal spiritual drive within me to be my very best. It gave me insight on identifying my personal wall and how I can overcome what life throws at me. It is a great resource and could be used as an indispensable reference to anyone who reads this great book—Well Done and Bravo!

~ **Karen Adams**, Montgomery County Maryland Public Schools

When I first picked up my wife's copy of this anthology, and read the title, I sensed it was a special project that would provide many other readers with hope, courage and inspiration. We never really know all that we will be faced with in life, but the courage and conviction of each of these writers sets the foundation on bouncing back from myriad issues — revealing it is how we approach life challenges that will make the difference.

Whether your life challenge involves the loss of a loved one, struggles of divorce, the trauma of past sexual abuse, emotions that come with receiving the news you (or a loved one) have a fatal disease or illness, the stress of financial difficulties, or fears and obstacles that have built up over a longer span of your life, THIS is an inspiring book to read.

The book was wisely designed with short, easy-to-read chapters, so you can pick it up at your convenience and read to your heart's content. I can guarantee, you will find yourself laughing, crying, relating to these women, and taking copious notes about how to draw on the lessons learned.

In the introduction, Antoinette Sykes tells us we will find "stories of bouncing back, tenacity, love, and of hope." She also shares her passion that this is a "better way to heal the world" in that God gave her this vision and experience to share with the world, to make it better, and to shed some light in a dark place.

~ T. R. Stearns, EdS

We have all heard stories about loss, infidelity, sickness, divorce, hard times, etc.; however this is not, in my opinion, the core of this book. These beautiful and vulnerable women are just like you and me... everyday people. They are Mothers, sisters, girlfriends, wives, fiancée, etc. They have offered themselves without prior knowledge to their circumstances to that "thing" which they all experienced'. They went through and came out smarter, happier, calmer, and more connected to others. In doing so, the shift I believe in each of their hearts and souls, is to help us navigate through life's bombshells [myself included].

All women, in my opinion, are connected. What's different here also, is that I immediately felt a connection with each story and realized this could be me. You might feel the same, or recognize your best girlfriend, your co-worker... someone you know has been there, done that... so to speak.

The stories reflect both joy and sorrow... you can hear the pain each one experienced in facing death, disappointments and setbacks. Praise should be given each author... for their break through and the new life they re-created. They have been able to sift through each challenge in their lives and reach a new plateau with strategies that we can use in our daily lives.

{An} Unsinkable Soul will warm your heart, your spirit and above all your soul!

~ Laura S. Chisholm, Proud Mother of Antoinette Sykes

Foreword

Has anything "awful" ever happened to you—anything that brought you to your knees?

Yes? Oh good!

Why on Earth would I say that? Because those "awful" things usually turn out to be the biggest gifts and blessings in our lives.

How do I know that?

As the Founder and Editor-in-Chief of *Law of Attraction Magazine*—and as a longtime personal and executive transformation coach—I've heard thousands of people's stories. I've also spent decades studying and teaching personal-growth and transformation material, and along the way, I've experienced many, many of my own breakthroughs, as well as those of countless other people.

And what I've witnessed, over and over again, is the biggest *breakthroughs* often follow the biggest *breakdowns!*

There's something about being brought to our knees that peels away all of the defenses that we've built up, all of the programming and "entrainment" that we've received from our parents, teachers, peers and the media. We finally are faced with the realization that the lies we've been telling ourselves are not true.

During that dark night of the soul, we finally realize that everything we've done up to this point in lives has brought us to exactly where we are, and where we are is so painful that we're willing to stop doing the same thing over and over again, expecting different results.

We're finally ready to choose something truly, completely and radically new.

What that "something" looks like can be very different for different people, and that's the beauty of this book. *{An}*

Unsinkable Soul is filled with empowering tales of people who've experienced profound breakdowns, and who have bounced back stronger, happier and more powerful than ever before.

Bouncing Back

Recognizing that we can — and do — bounce back stronger, happier and more powerful than ever before is *hugely* empowering. It's the core message of this book, and it's the core message of the visionary woman behind this book: Antoinette Sykes. When Antoinette and I first connected, I was impressed by the power of her passion and purpose. I could feel a deep resonance with her message, and I could feel the clarity of her inner knowing.

It's obvious that this book is a huge part of Antoinette's mission in this lifetime. Like many of us, Antoinette has been through a lot. She's seen a lot, and she's done a lot. She has blazed trails. She has hurdled obstacles. She has felt guided. And she has felt abandoned.

Occasionally, she also has been guided by the "cosmic 2x4."

What's a cosmic 2x4?

Well, a 2x4 is a large piece of wood that's typically used for building things. This loving, benevolent universe — to give us a big smack upside the head —uses a cosmic 2x4, metaphorically!

(If the term "universe" feels uncomfortable to you, please feel free to substitute God, or Source Energy, or Mother Nature, or whatever term resonates with you.)

So, why would a loving, benevolent universe smack us with a cosmic 2x4?

Because we weren't listening! I know from years of experience that this universe is always sending us gentle messages. But sometimes we ignore those messages. And so the universe turns up the volume and the messages get louder. And yet, many of us continue to ignore those messages. It's like we've got our hands over our ears, shouting, "La la la la! I can't hear you!"

So then the universe says, "OK, I'm doing this for your own good..." And, whack! We get smacked with a cosmic 2x4!

Now, for some of us, that looks like getting fired. For others, it looks like getting a sudden and debilitating physical ailment. This universe is infinitely creative, so of course it finds infinitely creative ways to get our attention.

Learning to Trust

Fortunately, we don't always require the cosmic 2x4. We simply need to learn to dance and play with the universe. We need to open up so that we can receive guidance in gentler and softer ways. A big part of that opening process involves learning to *trust* — to trust ourselves, trust the universe and trust in the *perfection* of each moment unfolding in our lives.

Now, I realize (oh, do I realize!) that sometimes it's hard to see that perfection in the midst of pain and fear. But I also know that, in time, we always gain perspective. And with perspective, we can look back and see the gift in our painful experiences.

When we allow ourselves to really and truly *know* this—to the depths of our beings—then we become able to trust the unfolding of life, even before we gain the perspective to see the perfection. Allowing ourselves to experience this level of trust helps tremendously when we're in the midst of the pain—when we can't imagine how something that hurts so much could possibly be for our best and highest good.

Trust allows us to remember, even in the midst of pain, that this loving and benevolent universe truly does have our back. This loving and benevolent universe truly does have our best interests at heart. In fact, this loving and benevolent universe is always bringing us *back home to ourselves,* back home to our inner power, our inner wisdom and our inner love and light.

So… how can we cultivate this profound trust?

You're holding one very powerful way in your hands right now! The authors of the 22 stories in this book have endured a wide variety of incredibly painful situations—the kind of situations that rocked them to their core. And yet, each of them bounced back. They rose above. They found the gift in the pain. And they came out the other side of these experiences more powerful, more self-honoring, more loving, more joyful and more alive!

And if they can do it, then you can too!

Sue Elliott

Founder and Editor-in-Chief of *Law of Attraction Magazine*
Executive and Personal Transformation Coach
LovingMyself.com
Irvine, California

Acknowledgements

This is a very grown up book, I must say. Then again, I've always been before my time. This I know. For that solid footing, my deepest thanks goes to my mama, who will forever be "my mama". While jokingly, she's always kidded that she would change her name, alas to me she will forever be my mama. Her status as 'my biggest fan' never grows boring with me. Her endless love and profound understanding without saying a word, leaves me speechless. I can only strive to be all that to my unborn offspring some day.

Many thanks to my family—each of you—remind me daily of who I am and what I'm made of. I do indeed know that I come from "good stock" via my blood DNA and my holy DNA. I love each of you more than words can say. It is because of your unwavering love and sheer candor that prepared me to face the world.

My dear friends that feel like family, my BFFs (Lisa, Tanya, Hillari, Roxy, and Paula), and my too-many-to-name VIP friends, you make me, remade me and shape me to know that blood doesn't only make family. I love each of you and as we grow old(er), we will still be fine as wine, fit and just pretty darn fabulous all around. It will be my honor to sip with you, serve up laughter and prayers with you. Over a cliff…

To the Duerson, Motley and Levell families (Clarence, Leon, JuElla, & Mary Sue), you were such a rock of unconditional love and support. Deep thanks and profound gratitude is what I hold dear in my heart for you forever.

Thanks to Karen, Tonya, Charles, Clyde and Barbara for every workout as your coach and personal trainer. You just didn't know how much it actually healed me.

I have one Sissy and she's the absolute best. I have one aunt, who is certainly the very best second mother a gal could have. Diva status is where you reign. Wendy and Aunt Ann, I love you. I love you. I love you.

Thank you to everyone who has ever read a blog post of mine, eBook, coached with me and heard me grab the mic and speak.

A huge heart felt thanks goes to Chip Chisholm, my Daddy-O, who is a man of many silent words, yet strong and mighty; and super cool. Thank you for definitively telling me, "This is not your fault. It had nothing to do with you. You will get through this". Without those words piercing my soul, I know my life would be different. I love you.

My literary team rocks; that's all. Thank you.

Dedication

This book is dedicated to my first responders' team (Mama, Chip, Lisa & Ray Charles). And anyone that has ever been in deep pain and didn't know a way out. May you hear the whisper that is loud to your soul and not to your ears. Ah, yes. That's it. The one that sounds familiar. That still small voice is calling you. It's your unsinkable soul. Please answer. Therein lies your protection, peace and power.

Be still and know that I am.

~ Psalm 46:10

Table of Contents

Introduction

Years ago… or shall I say since I was young, I always longed for a lovely man that was just for me. You know the one that only fairy tales tell of, minus the horse. There was one problem, where the heck was he? I knew deep down, I mean from every cell in my body that he existed. I wasn't too picky, although at times, I listened to others and succumbed to "something else" other than my own voice. Unfortunately, it only led to heartbreak and emptiness. That was not a good feeling, so when I met Dave and we clicked on every level, I was confident I wasn't just picky.

I also knew I wasn't silly for believing in my love dream.
I knew my prayers had finally been answered
and he knew his had been answered, too. What bliss!

As I sat to write of this story of Love, Loss & Liberation, I realized I had to invite others to share their respective stories of bouncing back, tenacity, love, and hope. What better way to heal the world? God gave me this vision and experience to share with the world, to make it better place, and to shed some light in a dark place. After all, isn't that what we're here for?

Writing this story has been no easy feat. In doing so, I've certainly rehashed all of my tears, fears and every other feeling associated with that love and loss. Nothing can ever prepare you for suicide and certainly not the suicide of your fiancé. Yet, there I stood, and here I stand, telling about it in a healthy, healing and heart-warming manner. My journey of healing, love and transparency are meant to sooth your pain, heal your soul and give you hope of moving beyond your current situation.

It's my intention that you find something that is tickling, relatable, strange yet familiar, and to walk away with a gem or two… or perhaps emerge a new you. As you read each story my desire is that you look deep within your heart and finally know where you belong, have the courage to move beyond the now, and create a new way of being. Because, as Oprah says, "What I know for sure is that some life events change you forever." You don't recognize the old you or the current you; the only thing for you to do is to fully embrace this newness and create a new way of being you. And you know what? That's quite all right. So, if you were waiting for permission – I give you permission. In fact, I insist on it.

As you prepare to read the stories on the following pages, I leave you with this prayer and these kind words. You are wonderful just as you are. You are beautiful and you are not your past. Everything that you have experienced up to this point has only prepared you for the transformation of your next chapter.

God, let angels whisper right now in the ear of the reader.
Wrap your protective wings through the tears and fears, for
full comfort. Mend hearts. Light the pathway for the new
journey and may peace fill their hearts. So it is. Amen.

Turn the page. Your life now begins.

XOXO

CHAPTER 1

Loss, Love & Liberation

Antoinette Sykes

Nothing, and I do mean no one thing or no one person, can ever prepare you for losing someone in this world, especially when suicide is the chosen route. For some, death is an accepted part of life, albeit painful, but a part of it, nonetheless. For others, it's this deep dark place that we dread and do not dare touch with our emotions until it imposes on an experience within our own circle of love. Then there is me... a person full of faith, full of passion for life, living in the Divine throughout my journey. Yet, when this death phenomenon happened, the wind was surely knocked from my stomach and everything seemed to simply stop—including my understanding, my solid-footed faith of my connection to the divine, and even who the heck I really was.

જાજાજી

I did have faith, but it seemed to morph into that of an intellectual knowing versus the deeply rooted feeling that was always with me... as close as my next breath. I missed that. I missed Dave. I missed me. And certainly I missed Him. Yet, through it all... tears, heartache, blunders and nights of soul bleeding, my love was wrapped up in this loss, but in the midst there was peace and liberation awaiting me. Ah, finally I found Him and me again. He loved me through the loss. He loved me through the love experience. And He led me to liberation again. And I am forever changed and forever free to BE. Throughout my journey of love, loss and liberation He never left me.

The Light on the inside of you is bright
enough for any darkness.
Shine your Light!

Love | Loss

February 17, 2010… I awoke at 6:30 A.M. as I normally did, taking those first steps to the bathroom and checking my phone for any missed text messages from my sweetie. *Hmmm, that was odd,* "Make sure my brain gets to the NFL brain bank," was what it said. Surely this totally confused me and yet, I automatically sensed something deeper and puzzling in the midst. My next calls to him would prove to be equally so; no answers to my normal love messages of, "Call me later," "I see you were up late," "I miss you," and so on. Off I went to get my day started and still no word or muster of my phone ringing, texts dinging. Absolutely nothing, and that was unbelievably odd.

It was about mid-morning while making make a trip to the bank, I wasn't able to round the corner before every bell-like cell in my body starting ringing loudly that something was awry, danger was in the midst and he was gone! I frantically drove back home, tears streaming down my face, my breath beyond elevated and my voice trembling as I called our condo-building manager to ask if he had seen Dave. Ron, the building manager, sensed my serious tone, even though at that point I was still somehow able to hold back the panic. Ron jokingly asked if I was planning the wedding and needing Dave's input. I said, Yes!" As I hung up, and Ron went to knock on our unit—I knew in my soul that my sweetie was gone. Moments later, but what felt like hours, Ron called urging me to get there ASAP.

"Angel, it doesn't look good."

"What did you see, Ron, just tell me", I screamed! He told me and the cries would not stop; I screamed and screamed and screamed for what seems like two years now... with thoughts running rampant through my mind.

It was indeed suicide. It was indeed a true text message of what I was to do with his brain. But, how — why?

Wait... we're getting married in a couple of months?

Wait... we just had Valentine's Day dinner together with lovely plans of our future.

Wait... I just heard your voice in prayer hours before the final text message came in.

Wait... I have so many questions and just make it stop – the pain, my spinning head, my whirlwind shake-up.

I want to laugh again and laugh with you.

I want to walk down the aisle to you, smiling at my beauty and me.

I want to feel safe again.

I want to see you and your thick mustache and baldhead.

I want to see you and smell your cigar aroma.

I want to dance to our song, or any song.

I want to walk the beach again gathering seas shells.

I want to count the many shapes of the clouds while walking outdoors.

I want to just have you once again in my face, just being.

I want to sip our favorite wine or share morning coffee time together.

I want to attend church together and pray as we part one another's presence.

I want to giggle with you or at you for no reason.

I want to experience your undoubting faith in me, and all that I seek to do.

I want to feel the strength, protection and unconditional love you exuded.

I want what you promised.

My wants and all our plans ceased on February 17, 2010, yet somehow I still manage to smile and have set you free in the process. And in letting go of you, I myself am free—freer than I've ever been. It was a damn hard journey, though, as my dreams of us slowly morphed into a true dream for a life of my own in which I had always believed. I see it all more clearly now... when we met life came alive in living color; it was God and it was good. It was my prayer being answered.

You were more than an answered prayer—you were a dream come true, my testimony, my God-sent angel—and together we were joined in a soul filled way before our physical encounter. It mattered not to me whether others may or may not have "gotten" it. I did. You did. God did. And with His guidance, I always win. And truth be told, loving you felt like winning a jackpot of limitless amounts of winnings. There was nothing to which to compare it; it just was divine love manifesting in you and through me. Thank you for saying yes to your soul. Thank you for loving me the way I needed. It has forever changed my life, awakened my purpose and healed my past—all to prepare me for the future—one filled with even more love in all areas of my life. I knew all along you existed well beyond my prayers and journal entries. I now also know you exist as my angel forever. So it is.

Liberation

I am free. I am love. I am peace. I am spirit forever. It wasn't until after your exit that these understandings truly rang true for me. You called me your Angel. I thought nothing of it at the time; it's a nickname that everyone calls me. Yet, there were times where those words simply transcended as they leapt from your lips. I knew it then. You knew it. God confirmed it. And now, I am reminded of it.

I now have the clarity that it's not just me that has this Divine quality; it's available within all of us. In the years leading up to meeting you, I didn't always listen to my still small voice. Without question or doubt, it seems we all embrace how the world just squeezes every bit of us to a point where the noise of life is the loudest. So in that moment, responding to the noise becomes the insane choice we make. I know you felt that in your last moments. The noise was too loud. You felt separate and alone from our Father. The noise was too loud for you to remember who you were and you simply wanted the pain to cease. I get it (*now*). No judgment, I just get it.

Those moments of insane choices that served me momentarily, always failed. So, did they ever really serve me? In this present moment, I'd say "No," but I do know every experience has a lesson for us to awaken to the remembrance of who we truly are. I did. I started to awaken upon meeting you. And since your exit, I have fully stepped through the Divine door. And it feels simply good, joyous and full of love.

What's most astounding now, although at times some outside circumstances appear bleak, blah and boldly scream a fearful reality, I finally sit in peace, in truth, in love and let myself be pulled to the Truth of who I AM. The essence of peace, truth and love works every time. It is because of the journey with you that I'm now able to boldly stand in my Truth and share that wisdom, truth and knowledge with others. It bleeds through my work, life and play. God has a way that I may never understand, but as I said at your memorial, "I have more questions than answers, but I still trust You". That one line summarizes my foundation. My mama and family laid the foundation early in my faith walk. I'm thankful I gladly accepted it to a new dimension or this story here about me... about you, would look totally different.

I am liberated! I love greater.
I see love in everyone and everything because God is love.

5

Thank you for a cracking open my heart and healing it all at the same time. Your presence then and now is simply all-good and all-God. So it is. Amen.

This is how I became Unsinkable and you can, too. Act upon the following steps frequently and adjust your perception where needed, and I guarantee you too, will discover your [Unsinkable] soul.

Have faith in God

Have faith in yourself, as you are one with God and nothing lacks in that awareness.

Dream; dream big and believe in your dreams.

Love big and give it away; it will come back to you.

Do something for someone else, big or small, it matters not. Simply do something with a pure heart.

Take care of your temple (body).

Know that only Love exists

You are just as God created you; whole and timeless.

Do something that makes you laugh... daily, deeply and moment-by-moment when needed. There within, lies your natural state.

Whatever situation you're in or have been in... it's a learning lesson that is meant to propel you forward; it is not meant to sink you.

Be still and hear that still small voice; it never leads you wrong.

Pray daily; meditate daily.

The poem that follows speaks to me... it was used in Dave's memorial program and it is a reminder or confirmation that you indeed are the master of your [Unsinkable] soul.

Invictus

~William Ernest Henley

Out of the night that covers me,
Black as the Pit from pole to pole,
I thank whatever gods may be
For my unconquerable soul.

In the fell clutch of circumstance
I have not winced nor cried aloud.
Under the bludgeoning of chance
My head is bloody, but unbowed.

Beyond this place of wrath and tears
Looms but the Horror of the shade,
And yet the menace of the years
Finds, and shall find, me unafraid.

It matters not how strait the gate,
How charged with punishments the scroll.
I am the master of my fate:
I am the captain of my soul.

ೞೲ

About the Author

Transformation Life Coach, Antoinette Sykes, helps others transform, transition and triumphantly live the life they've only imagined of freedom and unlimited happiness, with a fervent belief that you can live the life you truly dream of and not settle if you trust all things are possible through the one that created you.

As {An} Unsinkable Soul, Antoinette uses the knowledge derived from a BS in Psychology, MBA in Marketing, and a Subconscious

Reconditioning Life Coaching certification... combined with life experiences as an elite workplace leader and survivor of two layoffs and losing her fiancé to suicide, to smilingly help others transform, transition and triumphantly live the life of freedom and unlimited happiness they've only imagined.

At any given time you can find Antoinette, who is a lover of life and all things self-help, living to her image of being ridiculously happy... inspiring the masses via speaking, social media or one of her coaching programs, and singing with her hairbrush as the microphone!

She can be contacted at http://AntoinetteSykes.com.

CHAPTER 2

From Fear to Fabulous

Teresa Bruni

A story about a 10-year journey overcoming chronic illness

I found myself lying in bed in the middle of the night awake and wondering how I got here. It was 1996 and I was sick, very sick. I had been on full disability for nearly seven years. *How did this happen? How did I get here?* I felt completely lost and overwhelmed with despair. I felt powerless. I didn't recognize my life. I didn't even recognize myself. And I didn't know what to do.

ଔଚ୦ଚ

Prior to this illness I had always been healthy and physically strong. I had never been in the hospital, never had a broken bone or even stitches, other than when my wisdom teeth were extracted as a teen. The flu would go around the entire office twice but I wouldn't get it. I had been healthy and strong. The burning questions were, how did I get here and how do I get back?

I was lost. Completely lost, living in an unfamiliar world full
of struggle, worry and fear.
It seemed that no matter how hard I tried I could not get well.

My physical strength preceding my illness was above average. In the summer months I swam nearly a mile a day and lifted weights and practiced yoga year round. I could leg press 175 pounds with ease. I was socially active, too. In addition to my corporate job I served on two community committees and played volleyball on the corporate team. But now I found myself suffering from fatigue, debilitating fatigue that had become unmanageable. My body ached all the time, my physical strength was significantly diminished, and I couldn't sleep. I suffered from low-grade fevers, swollen glands, chronic sinus infections, severe joint pain, headaches and sore throats. But worst of all, I couldn't concentrate. It was like having the flu 24/7 for seven years. Was I going to die? No. But some days I wished I would just to end the misery.

When I first started having symptoms I asked my doctor for a complete physical. Nothing stood out in the lab tests and my body was so physically strong that my long-time personal physician told me there was nothing wrong with me. He handed me a prescription and sent me for stress management. Although I thought he must be mistaken, I trusted him and followed his instructions. I filled the prescription and made an appointment to see the "stress management specialist." Looking back now, I have to laugh when I realize that what he prescribed was an antidepressant and the stress management specialist he sent me to was a shrink (psychologist).

In his defense, I suppose someone who is deeply immersed in the science of medicine, who is on the lookout for proof and finding none, may not see many other options for a condition such as what I was experiencing. Having never suffered from anything that couldn't be fixed by a short course of antibiotics, I didn't know what to expect from doctors. I certainly wasn't experienced at being ill and I didn't know how to manage this serious situation... serious in that this was affecting my health, my body, my career – my life.

Despite his diagnosis I knew there was something wrong; I was sick. I was calling in sick from my corporate job two to three days per week because I couldn't get out of bed. I couldn't sleep and I couldn't stay awake. Even the most basic tasks became challenging.

After nearly two years of going from doctor to doctor to find out what was wrong with me, I was fortunate enough to be directed to an Immunologist at the University of Medicine and Dentistry in Newark, New Jersey. His specialty at the time was Pediatric Immunology and Infectious Diseases and he was a leader in his field. I literally had to beg to get an appointment with him and when the day arrived, I found myself at a hospital in Newark surrounded by a sea of chronically ill children; some terminally ill. Little kids walking around while pushing their IV stands, some bald from chemo. It was a heartbreakingly devastating experience. I felt surrealistic; like living in a nightmare.

The doctor and his staff examined me, drew four large vials of blood and prepared to run every test imaginable including HIV. At that time HIV was a hush, hush phrase. If you even mentioned it, people who knew you for years might refuse to eat with you or even touch you ever again. It was a fear-provoking time.

I was officially diagnosed with Chronic Fatigue Syndrome (formally known as Epstein-Barr virus) and was directed to other doctors for treatment. The blessing of finally having a diagnosis washed over me and gave me hope even though there was no known treatment. Everything was experimental. Having never been seriously ill until now, I did what the doctors told me to do. I trusted that they had the answers I needed to get well. I was given pills to sleep at night and pills for energy in the morning, pills for the headaches and pills for the joint pain. I had three major surgeries during those years, two sinus surgeries and a tonsillectomy. Pretty serious stuff for someone like me who, prior to this, only went to the hospital to visit other people.

I couldn't work; my corporate career was on hold. I couldn't read for long periods because I couldn't concentrate. Everything – and I mean everything – was a struggle. I was losing hope of ever recovering and felt a complete loss of control over my own life. My new career was one of doctor visits (two to five per week) and insurance forms. Being on disability reduced my income by forty percent and I was exhausting my savings. The meager Social Security Disability yearly increase was not keeping up with inflation and I worried daily over how I would pay the bills. The simplest pleasures like a magazine or a pack of gum were outside my budget. Life basically sucked.

Little did I know, I was on a nearly ten-year long journey
that would lead me to the depths of chronic illness and then to
the miracle of recovery.

After nearly seven years of this insanity, I woke one day with renewed determination. It was clear to me that the doctors didn't have a cure. As much as I trusted them and was hopeful, I realized they couldn't cure me. They could only treat my symptoms. Seeing only two possible choices, continue to live this way forever or find my way back to health, I became determined to find my own answers.

I had my work cut out for me and I wasn't sure where to begin. I read as much as I could with my limited concentration and I did as much research as possible. Unfortunately the Internet was not an accessible resource like it is now. Instead, I found myself surrounded with books on healing of every type… including mind-body medicine, nutrition, natural healing, spiritual healing, and conventional medical books. But there was still something missing. I wasn't sure what it was.

I tried to be strong and live a normal life, only to suffer setbacks that could last for days or even weeks. One day I decided to surrender, to come to an acceptance of where I was. I always thought surrender meant giving up so I resisted it, but it doesn't. Surrendering allowed me to be completely present and to acknowledge exactly where I was. It provided a huge sense of relief. Surrendering felt good.

It was as if someone handed me a map clearly marked with an arrow that said, "You are here."

Too often people in situations like this are afraid to surrender. They think surrender means giving up but it doesn't. Surrender simply means acceptance. That's all.

I read a lot about how our emotions affect our health but I wasn't convinced. I was hardheaded and would tell anyone who would bring up the subject that my body was my body and my emotions were my emotions. They were, in my opinion, completely separate and my emotions had absolutely no effect on my health. I believed my body was breaking down for some other reason; a physical reason. I thought it had to be an outside force that caused my body to become weakened and then ill, like maybe polluted air or water, or food that lacked nutrition. I was wrong.

Looking back now it's easy for me to see the connection. As I started to work on my emotional health and began to release my fears (and fear takes many forms) I began to recover.

I had been through a painful divorce just prior to getting sick. Actually, I went through two divorces; one from my husband of seven years and one from my abusive family. I was raised in an abusive household. My parents were always arguing and my father physically abused my mother on at least one occasion. My most vivid memory was when I was about three or four years old, I think. I have managed to block out much of my childhood, but not that night.

As the argument between my parents escalated it started to become physically violent. Despite having five older siblings, I found myself hiding alone under a bed... and utterly terrified. When the torment was over my mother found me. During the argument she threatened to leave and when she rescued me from under the bed I said, 'Mommy, if you leave, will you please take me with you?"

By the time I was nine years old I had been subjected to emotional, physical, verbal and mental abuse. I was also sexually abused by the youngest of my three older brothers. All that abuse would last for years... diminishing my self-worth to nearly zero. I didn't feel worthy of anything as an adult. I thought I was a bad person because, in my logical mind, only bad people were treated this way. Even at my corporate job I felt like a fraud. I felt that if they knew who I really was I'd be asked to leave.

I vowed at an early age to never have children because in my reality the world was a horrible place with bad outweighing the good 10 to 1. Who in their right mind would want to bring a child into this world to suffer like I had?

It's no surprise that I ended up in a bad marriage. I thought I had married my best friend but once the marriage was sealed I became his property. The emotional and mental abuse began almost immediately. Years later, when physical abuse became a threat, I left. I wasn't accepting any of that as part of my life. I felt completely betrayed by the person I loved and trusted the most. The very person to whom I had freely handed my heart returned it to me completely shattered. I was beyond devastated and I questioned my ability to ever trust again.

Walking away and divorcing everyone who had ever mistreated me seemed like a logical answer. I thought, "Get away from them and the pain will stop." But it didn't. Failing to deal with the underlying issues of anger, shame, rage, hurt, betrayal, abandonment and a devastated self-esteem would take its toll and eventually cause me to become chronically ill.

It was time to deal with all of that and reclaim my self-worth if I wanted to get well.
It was time to take back control of my life.

Another thing that I did was to flush all the drugs from my system. I realized I was at a point where I couldn't distinguish the difference between the side effects of the medications I was taking and the actual symptoms of my illness. I only took the medications that were absolutely necessary. For example, if I had an infection I took antibiotics. This would allow me to recognize my real symptoms and begin to manage those using treatments other than pills whenever possible.

(PLEASE NOTE: I do not recommend that anyone reading this stop their medications without consulting their doctor first and making an informed decision!)

I began to use a combination Eastern and Western medicine – taking the best from both practices. I interviewed my doctors before hiring them. After all, this was "my" body and "my" health we were talking about. I questioned the medical treatments offered to me; I researched and made informed decisions on what I felt was best for me… I took control.

Eventually my doctors sent me for physical therapy. This was a treatment of which I approved. I'll never forget that first day. It was an hour's drive up the New Jersey Parkway and because of my limited ability to concentrate; this drive was extremely stressful and exhausting. When I finally met with the physical therapist my resting heart rate was 120 beats per minute. No wonder I was exhausted! My heart was beating as if I was running a marathon. Treatment began with only five minutes of exercise and five minutes of rest. This was quite the contrast for the physically strong person who once swam three miles in one day. I recall the lifeguards jokingly asking me if I was ever coming out of the pool.

I never felt I had control over anything in my life. I had become a victim to life's circumstances. Beginning to take control was a big step for me – and a crucial one! I started taking a good look within and listening to my intuition, my inner voice. I began to meditate and visualize. I had a daily practice of visualizing myself as strong and healthy. I had a clear picture in my mind of what that would look and feel like.

I also began to engage in a process called mirror talk. This is where you sit in front of a mirror, look yourself deep in the eyes and have a heartfelt conversation with yourself. In the beginning it was a difficult process and extremely painful. At first, I didn't even recognize myself in that mirror, but over time and with great patience and empathy for myself I was able to say, "I love you. You are worthy." I was often overcome with emotion while doing this work, which was a clear indication of the depth of the issues I faced, but in time it became easier and easier. I was beginning to heal my soul and comfort my inner child.

The effects of all those years of abuse had left a deep wound in my heart and had caused me to completely mask my soul, my inner guidance system. When a child is subjected to abuse or horrific events and they are not dealt with, the soul of the child begins to get masked over. Inherently the child knows that the abusive treatment is wrong but doesn't have the intellectual capacity to deal with it so the child does the only thing he/she knows to do… rationalize the behavior by developing false beliefs such as, "It must be my fault, I must not be worthy." There is no other rational explanation in a young child's mind.

I would soon discover that it would only be through forgiveness of everyone, myself included, that I could recover and reclaim my purpose, direction, clarity, joy, and self-esteem and begin to remove the mask from my soul and relearn to trust my inner guidance system. Slowly but surely I began to regain my health and eventually made a full recovery. It took nearly three years.

I believe no single treatment would have worked. It was only with a combination of all my treatments that I recovered. It was my job to get well and I took it seriously. But the most important treatment of all was dealing with the emotional baggage I had neatly packed away in a large trunk, layer upon layer, and carried with me everywhere since childhood.

What I needed more than anything for my recovery
was to regain my self-worth and my value as a person,
something with which we are all born.

Since this experience, I have become a firm believer that each and every one of us has all the answers we need inside us. It's what I call "internal truths." You were born with them; we all were. It's just a matter of learning how to tap into them again. How do I know this? In the years following my recovery, I have read about many of the self-treatments, emotion-based techniques and visualization methods, which I had discovered on my own. How could I have possibly discovered them before someone else introduced them to me? There is only one possible answer. It had to come from within. For example, the mirror talk process... I discovered it one day while I was brushing my teeth. I simply looked deeply into my own eyes. I saw something there that I didn't recognize and I continued to explore it. No one told me about mirror talk and I didn't read about it until years after my recovery; the same with the visualization exercise I developed for myself.

Beginning to trust myself, following my instincts,
my intuition and gut feelings, is what lead me to the

answers I needed to get well;
the answers that had always been there.

This experience also taught me that chronic physical conditions and chronic illness are caused by prolonged chronic, unresolved fear. As I mentioned earlier, fear comes in many forms: anger, resentment, rage, judgment (including self-judgment), impatience, hatred, blame, self-loathing, jealously, and so on. The effects of chronic fear are depression, insecurity, over-achieving, perfectionism, guilt, worry, unworthiness, grief, depression, despair, powerlessness, and hopelessness. Chronic and acute fear not only keeps you from living to your fullest potential, it takes a physical toll on your body. Once these fears are faced and dealt with, which is not always an easy process, the body is allowed to heal. Many others and I are living proof of this.

Today I can truly appreciate this experience for all that it has taught me about life. That's what forgiveness does. It allows you to see the gift tucked deep inside a tragic situation. Without all my life experiences, good and bad, I wouldn't be the person I am today. And now it is my life's purpose and my driving passion to enlighten others with the knowledge I have gained. It is my mission to show others how to reach deep down inside and tap into the power that has always been within; to hand them the roadmap marked with two arrows, one that says, "You are here" and another that says, "This is the way out."

Every person is born with enormous value and purpose, and a remarkable, dependable, never failing internal guidance system. There are no exceptions. Every person possesses these inherent qualities and gifts; internal truths. And no person has the right to inflict abuse on another in any form, to tear down someone's self-worth or cause major destruction to another's heart and soul. But when one can come to the understanding that it is the abuser who is truly disconnected from self, forgiveness comes more easily and then healing can begin.

One of the major lessons I learned from this experience, and one that I would like to share is... our bodies are our compass. When we go off track emotionally, we get physical signals to alert us. It could be anything from a common skin rash to a sore joint or muscle. Ignore the signals and they become worse – eventually causing us to have accidents, develop chronic conditions that require surgery or making us seriously ill. Our bodies try to get our attention and if we ignore the signals we then pay the price physically. Fear, anger, rage, blame, self-blame... all those emotions (and more) must be dealt with and the sooner the better. It doesn't take a barrage of assaults over the course of many years like I experienced. It could be one single experience that shatters your heart, diminishes your trust, or causes you to question your own self-worth.

I often describe my journey as nearly seven years heading down a dark tunnel and another three years heading back towards the light. I am not only grateful, but incredibly proud to say that I have been healthy, back to work full-time, and living a more fully engaged life since 1999, celebrating 15 years of "renewed self!" Some of my family relationships have been repaired and some have not, but it is not due to a lack of forgiveness on my end. The truth of the matter is, some toxic relationships just have to end and I'm okay with that. I am completely worthy of love and respect and I am not willing to accept anything less. Is life perfect? No and I don't expect it to be, but what I have now that I was starved for in the past is control over my destiny, and that feels amazing.

Today I am a dedicated and purpose-driven certified
professional life coach, a conscious energy master
practitioner, speaker, and author.
I am dedicated to improving lives wherever I go.

Whether your fears are holding you back from the next level of success in your career or have you locked within a prison, a prison taking the form of a health crisis, there is help available to you. There are people who care and understand, and who have the skills to help you. I urge you to remain hopeful and seek them out starting today.

You are not the servant of your body. You are the master!
~Teresa Bruni

ೞೞ

About the Author

Teresa Bruni, who specializes in creating life transformations, is on a mission; to assist her clients in reaching for higher goals and living fuller, richer lives by identifying and breaking through the blocks that keep them playing small. Teresa is a born teacher and is driven by her purpose to improve the lives of others. Teresa is a Certified Professional Coach (CPC), a certified Energy Leadership Index Master Practitioner (ELI-MP), an eWomen Network Premier Success Coach, author, speaker, and the founder of "Less Fear, More Flow." According to Teresa, *"A great day for me is a series of attentive listening experiences in which I uplift others with positivity, enthusiasm, laughter and joy!"* Learn more about Teresa and her work at http://teresabruni.com.

CHAPTER 3

From Numb to Awakened

Kevra Cherne

When I was asked to write a chapter in this book to share a bounce-back story I have to be honest, I really thought to myself, "What the hell do I have to share?" I think many of us have our lives. And they are just "our lives." Nothing of significance to us, because it is all we know. You know what I mean? So, despite constant objections from my ego, I'll share with you my experiences in life… in the hopes it will help or console or motivate a few of you in a positive way.

⊰⊱⊰⊱

My biological father is a rapist. This is a fact I grew up with. As matter of fact as, "We're having chicken for dinner." It was just common knowledge to which no drama was fed into in the years I remember as I grew up. To be honest, I didn't think much about it. It just was. With that knowledge, however, on a subconscious level came the thinking, "I am less than because of whom my father is."

You see, my mom and he were married and while she was still pregnant with me he raped a woman and was sent to prison. I'm not sure which confuses me more, raping another human or studying to become a pastor and raping a person. I've still not figured that out.

My mom was a young mom; at 18 she was pregnant with my brother. I get (now) that she did everything she knew how to do and the very best she could have at the time.

I remember nothing of husband #2… just a bit more of #3.

Most vividly, I remember hiding in my room under a dark oak desk my brother and I had both gotten for Christmas one year. We had either just moved in or I was rearranging my room a bit because I remember this desk being in the middle of the floor of my room at an angle. I recollect hearing a loud, deep male voice exploding and I recall going under my desk to hide. I remember the screams and cries that came from my brother's room after that – as he received yet another beating from our stepfather. He got beat a lot, and I'm not sure my brother has ever recovered fully.

I, on the other hand, figured out at a young age how to be quiet, blend in, and do well in school. Don't rock the boat! I also remember getting a job at an early age, 13 or 14. I loved the feeling of getting out of the house and earning my own money! It was actually the first place where I think I really started to experiment with that question so many of us go through our lives trying to figure out, "Who am I?"

Thankfully, my mom met a man whom I grew comfortable referring to as my Dad. This amazing man truly acted as a white knight like the storybooks always promised… though I didn't see him in this capacity at all for the first year. He came in and took me out of this place I called "home and normal" and showed us a new way to live; I was 15 then. We moved once that school year to a different city, and I was so angry with both of my parents. Here I was… a normal, confused, angry teenager who got yanked out of what reality I knew and thrust into something I didn't understand. For the first year I can't say I was very nice to him or my mom. To this day, what I remember of that time is that he loved me through it; something I had never experienced before. Somewhere along those lines I grew to love him like a Dad and we had a strong bond. Until his passing, he was the referee between my mom and me.

As a young adult, freshly graduated from high school, I went to college as only I would, four days after graduating high school to begin summer term at St. Cloud State University, about two hours from home. Little did I know that summer classes were often only attended by students studying abroad, so I found myself in my own dorm room surrounded by an Oriental community of young people who cooked smelly fish and Raman noodles!

Going off to college I had $75 in my pocket, and plans to change the world. Well, not really, but to find something outside of me in a huge capacity. Needless to say, I needed to find a job. I was willing and able and found myself applying to be a bus driver. At the tender age of 18, there I was, driving 50 plus young people to school.

I would say the majority of my twenties was spent living my shadow life. You know your shadow side... the one where you don't necessarily live in your highest potential? For most women, I imagine, it is a time of learning your limits, learning what gets you things (attention, men, jobs) and what doesn't.

And then I found myself at the age of 34, knowing I was at the end of my marriage with my husband. Married for just a few years, and in a relationship upwards of 14 years together. What had happened? In that time I had gotten my degree, had two children, had a decent job with excellent benefits and even left that job to start my own company. For some reason, I still felt... empty.

23

I realized I had lived my whole life until that point relying on someone else to make me happy.

That's not how it works.

Many people ask me when I felt that shift in myself. And, until now, I knew roughly the time of life, but not the moment. The pivotal moment was when I read Tony Robbins book, *Awaken the Giant Within.* I had never felt so alive! I felt a fire in my belly. I felt my blood flowing through my veins again. I felt my brain going into overdrive. I felt passionate once again – or for the first time – it doesn't matter.

I. Just. Felt.

It was almost as if I had never cried in my whole life or laughed in my whole life until that book opened me; that's what I felt like. I was finally opened; awakened!

I'm not sure if that makes me Unsinkable or not. One thing I know is once you're opened – or awakened – you cannot go back to being numb. In my enlightenment, I found a new philosophy: "Once you're aware, you have a choice to change." So change I did.

In the spring of 2011 my ex-husband and I were still together. I attended a three-day Holistic Exhibition where about 40 other vendors would be in Milwaukee. With my accounting business in tow – because all businesses need an accountant, right – it was there that I had some of my own Awakenings. I sat in on workshops – from energy healing to crystals and anything in between – completely fascinated.

And, with each moment of excitement came a reality-check moment of, "He will never go for it." In those moments, I knew our marriage was really, really over. I returned home and told my husband I wanted a divorce. We agreed I would stay until school was out so the kids would have the summer to adjust. Within two weeks of that my son fractured his arm and two weeks after that my dad (#4) passed away.

Life is often fast and furious.

I will never forget the day I was leaving my ex-husband telling me, "Grass isn't greener on the other side of the fence." I paused and thought to myself, "Huh?" and kept on moving. In those short weeks of announcing the divorce, my dad passing and the actual move out of my home I realized the great serendipitous nature of the Universe. Have you experienced it? The reality that when you really claim something in life, things outside of your consciousness show up to support you?

I'd had a client for several years that owned several rental properties and had become a friend. It was to her I turned for rentals; she knew exactly, when I asked if she had any rentals open, which one would be the perfect one. The one she selected… was perfect!

On June 11th I moved into that little white, two-story corner house and found me for probably the first time in my life. I enjoyed being alone with myself and found I was stronger alone, than in a relationship where I was leaking need onto someone else.

So, not to sound all filled with wisdom with you all, but the message I feel compelled to start is, "You must learn to love yourself, no matter what situations you get yourself into or out of – or those uncontrollable events life serves you. Love yourself through it all. Love yourself first. Before you can love your children, before you can love a partner, before any of it, you must learn to love yourself. Unfortunately, this seems not to be something we are taught, especially as women. For those of you that are mothers, be conscious you are teaching this to your children; especially your girls.

It was also during this time my business was shifting from my being an accountant – entering into more of a teaching realm. I started working with women more on why they continue to not have money or make money or keep money. You guessed it! A lot of them were not in supportive relationships and didn't think they deserved it. Through this work I actually tapped into many issues I didn't know I carried about being the daughter of a convicted rapist. On a conscious level I believed I could be happy—but only to a certain point. I could have money but only to a certain point. I could be loved but only to a certain point. There was a glass ceiling hovering over my own happiness because of where I came from. How many of you can relate to that?

Today, I'm happy to share with you... I am remarried, with a total of six children and three dogs. Today, I both know and love myself; I know how to capture the opportunities for growth... each and every day, and to be who I am all the time.

Take me or leave me, no deal to me!

I have continued my professional path toward helping an increasing number of women set up businesses with the kind of foundation that ensure success for them, with more money and more happiness in their lives.

Every day is a beginning, where we choose look our demons or obstacles in the face each – stand-off with them and say, "Today is mine." Then... listen to yourself, and follow your heart about what is best for you. Amen.

"Do the thing that scares you every day." -Eleanor Roosevelt

CRWRU

About the Author

Kevra Cherne, founder of Money Freedom Solutions, works with heart centered women entrepreneurs to bring Spirit and Business together to create a six-figure lifestyle. With over 15 years in the finance field, Kevra brings her proven techniques, systems and business know-how, with no guess-work and no nonsense, to those who admit to longing for more structures, systems and a streamlined way to run a healthy business. A light-hearted pragmatist, Kevra can easily be contacted at http://moneyfreedomsolutions.com/

CHAPTER 4

Unsinkable Me

Laura Clark

I loved camp. I was so at home playing tennis, hiking, swimming, weaving and laughing after taps with my tent mates. I was encouraged, and indeed felt, that I could do anything and be anything. Beyond camp activities, the light breezes, the cool lake, the warm sun and the moss in the woods somehow always made me feel like I was supported, strong and indeed loved. They were bliss-filled days.

〜〜〜

"I just can't anymore…." "There's no hope…." And "It's so bad, I just can't breathe." These were the words I had come to tell myself over and over and over again as a young adult. Life was very different since those carefree days of camp. I worried too much. I felt unappreciated. I had spiraled downward.

I found myself lying on the floor. I had a book on my belly and he was telling me to just breathe. "Relax and take a deep breath," I heard him saying. I couldn't. With each breath I said, "I just can't. There's no hope…" The more, I would try the more anxious I became and the harder it was to breath. Finally, I said, "I just can't do this."

And, with that, I got up and left my psychologist's
office and sobbed.

That night, I decided it was time to face facts. After twenty years of saying to myself "I don't know what's wrong with me." "I don't want to be like this. I don't want to be like her." I faced the fact that I was. Indeed, I had at that time in my eyes, become just like her: my mother. I was in the depth of yet another depression just like my mother. And, this episode was worse than all the others combined.

After a few very dark nights filled with sobbing and sitting in front of a potpourri of pill bottles, I went back to my psychologist's office. Sheepishly, I said to him "I get it. I have depression. I surrender. But that doesn't mean I have to be like her. Does it?" He smiled. "No, Laura, it doesn't and you have just discovered the keys to your kingdom." We tried the breathing exercise again and for the first time in my life, I began to breathe.

My mother had battled depression all her life. It was probably why I liked camp so much. I was able to get away from it. I had always tried to be the good girl (mostly failing in my behavior), and the older I got, the more I tried to make it better for her. If I was good at school, if I achieved on the athletic field, if I had friends, she'd have to be happy, right? At least that's what my inner child thought.

Of course, depression is so much more than that. And, what you resist in your mind will persist in your world. I had spent so much time and energy trying not to recognize depression, trying not to understand it, but to avoid it. I had resisted so much by "not wanting to be like her." Focusing on all of this, I put my genetic pre-disposition self into a situational place of isolation, discomfort and discontent that depression ultimately came upon me. I felt that depression was my birthright.

At that point in life, I was continuing to be the good girl. It wasn't working. I had worked hard, did well in school and was on the career path – doing what I thought I 'should' be doing. I was making choices that I thought would make my mom proud of me. The big kicker was that no one knew I had depression. I would go to work and do a good job. I thought I enjoyed my work but I was really just trying to escape my depression. At work, I didn't have to face my depression. At home, I was alone. I hated being alone. At home, my self-talk would take me deeper into depression.

So, I chose not to be around it as much as possible. I would work so hard that I had no energy and by the time I got home, I was so tired that I would just crash on the couch. You can be tired but you can never get away from your own inner voice. I would hear them loud and clear. Voila, I had become my mother. See, that's where she spent much of her time, on the couch.

What my psychologist did when he handed me the 'keys to my kingdom' was in essence tell me, "You are indeed not your mother. You, Laura, can come through depression differently than your mom, with different results, because you are not your mother." I was seeking support and tools that she would not.

That was twenty years ago; what I didn't know then was the significance of that 'little' exercise and the lesson I learned that day. It not only had a profound impact on my own healing, but it had profound influence on getting me 'back to camp.' Indeed, it had a direct impact on my discovery of the true purpose in my life.

Depression is an invisible illness that can have devastating effects. It places a shadow over one's life, one's relationships and one's career path. Its treatment has progressed significantly over the course of my lifetime. Resources are available.

There is a balance over how western medicine treats the disease and how eastern medicine supports it so that one can embrace their own inner joy and live on purpose with greater success and ease. Yet, depression hurts. It's an isolating illness because when living with it one feels so very alone. Everyone has bad days where their mood is off and they just wait till tomorrow because tomorrow typically is better. Anyone with depression thinks that one bad day leads into another and it feels as though there is no hope of every having a good day again.

There was once a stigma to having depression. People simply did not understand how someone could not just 'snap out of it.' Slowly, this veil is being lifted. Yet, in today's pressurized world, people are slow to seek help and accept support because of their own perception with this stigma. They are slow to accept that living can go from seeing the proverbial glass as half empty (indeed empty) to seeing it as half full (indeed overflowing.) I'm a living and breathing example that when you do seek help, when you do accept support and when you learn to breathe and understand your own inner strength and wisdom, life becomes full again. It becomes brighter and indeed, can be lived in joy.

That's what I did on that day so many years ago... tap into the energy of my breathing. Of course, I didn't know that then. All I knew was that I saw a glimmer of hope and I attached my spirit to it and never looked back. What I did on that day was stop the downward spiral of the energy of depression. I started the work. I started to make choices. Choices about how I thought about myself. Choices about how I wanted to live my own life.

I began by just breathing. And, with that first breath, I moved forward into following a path of joy for myself. And, that's when I saw the light at the end of the tunnel. Of course, changes take time. Many empowerment gurus say that you can just choose differently. Sounds simple enough, yes? But, if you have never been taught how to choose – how to really make empowered choices that are best for you – then, often you make choices that have you continue to follow the energy of depression and spiral downward. I was making choices that way. I made choices that were not good for me. Choices based on what I thought other people wanted me to make.

So, I took time to begin to self-correct my inner chatter. I took time to learn how to listen to my inner guidance system. And, I began with the choice to get support and to get help. My healing started off very traditionally with western medicine. It grew into one that found a balance between western and eastern medicine principles. Finally, my healing rests in a place that is its own. I discovered how to shine light on my own soul and read its compass that navigates this journey that I call my life.

It wasn't always easy. There were tears. Those tears, however, allowed for layer upon layer of poorly created belief systems to be shed. With each layer shed, I see a brighter horizon and future. And indeed this healing continues. As I grow and journey forward, new roadblocks are hit: tears happen again... life doesn't stop, does it?

What is different now is that I am able to recognize my emotions for what they are. I am able to quickly self-correct my inner talk when it begins to take a wrong turn. I am able to quickly ground my emotions, challenge the old thought (the "I cant's") and create new, powerful beliefs in alignment with my soul's purpose. This allows me to navigate past these roadblocks with much less effort than I ever was able to before.

Two decades from when I took that first 'adult' breath, I am now living a life that is grounded. I am living a life filled with joy at any given moment. During these two decades, my life has transitioned a lot. Here are some of my successes: I quit my job, moved home, came to terms with my mother and indeed began to "in-joy" time with her despite her own depression. Empathy works. I have started not one but two successful businesses. I am in love with an incredible man and our life together is joy-filled.

The tears and the work were worth it. My heart-felt desires in the work that I now do blossomed from them. I was able to align what made me happy as a child with who I am now and follow what I know to be my soul's path. I am living a life that is based on those principles I learned at camp. I am allowing the earth, the air, the water and the fire elements to be my guide to my own inner wisdom.

I'm meant to be 'at camp' always. What this means is to take the lessons that are air, water, fire and earth and not only use them in my own life but also share them with others so that they can quickly overcome bad days and move into a life that supports them. Where they can easily shine a light on their own soul and follow its wisdom as the compass that inspires their lives to passion and purpose and living in-joy.

Life happens. Depression hurts. Bad days come. Each can easily stop you from living a path designed for as much joy as you desire and, indeed, deserve. Before blue days fall into darker ones, you can find ways to live in joy. The possibilities are within us at all times.

With the right support, and with the right tools, you can make choices that lead you to living an inspired life. It is my deepest hope that you give yourself the gift of joy by uncovering your soul's wisdom and following it to a life on purpose and in joy.

Where Intention Goes, Energy Flows.
~ Denise Linn

ೞ೫౸ಬ

About the Author

Laura Clark, founder of Soul Wise Living, helps others re-align their energies for Abundance and Prosperity through her unique R.E.A.P™ Clarity & Success System... helping them find personal wisdom hidden behind years of listening to inaccurate information about themselves. Drawing from her own life experiences and the coach's training she received during her own journey, Laura uses private coaching, VIP Private Intensive Retreats, Group Wisdom Retreats and tele-courses to teach spiritual awakening tools to shift her clients from overwhelm to stress-less living, from fears and self-doubt to moving soulfully forward in clarity, success and joy. She can be reached at

http://www.soulwiseliving.com/.

CHAPTER 5

From Pain to Purpose

Serita Diana

I wasn't always a success. I didn't always believe I could succeed. In fact many times I have failed. I have been knocked down personally and professionally… again and again. I was bullied, sexually abused, and divorced. I got sick and had to leave promising jobs; I've even been fired due to the "company re-aligning" and there was no place for me in that re-alignment, and I lost some of the most important people in my life. I overcame it all because I walked the path I was on and didn't give up. But before I tell you how I got where I am I have to tell you where I was.

જ્ઞઉઝ

In 2003 my father had been having some minor health issues and his mother, my grandmother, was in the nursing home. I mention this because these are two of the people in my life to which I had been closest. That is where I felt the earth stop. My parents came to tell me how the test results were for my father and in the same sentence I found out he was terminally ill, and I was also told my grandmother had less than a week to live. I kept myself together as best I could while my parents were at my home and as soon as they left I took off for the basement at a run. I wanted to be alone when I fell apart because that is exactly what I knew was going to happen. I was 28 years old and I wasn't ready to lose either of them.

I didn't make it to the basement. My legs simply gave out and I collapsed on the floor fighting to breathe, with tears streaming down my face. I had dealt with a lot, but to me this was simply incomprehensible. A life without them was beyond anything I had imagined. Bit-by-bit I began functioning again, but in it all I closed up within myself and didn't let anything touch me for quite a while. Grandma died in April of that year, just two weeks before her 90th birthday. Dad was going to all the doctors he was scheduled to see for idiopathic pulmonary fibrosis. As for me... I had already used Google to find all I could about the dreaded disease and already knew before the doctors ever told him that there was no treatment or cure. The only hope was a lung transplant. I found myself walking and talking, but I was far from fine.

I had grown up with faith in God and nothing had ever shaken that faith. I grew up knowing I could take anything to God because he was my heavenly father. So to me it was perfectly natural that roughly a year after we learned all this about my father and grandmother I just blew up. I was like an unruly teenager. I was driving down the road and I started out talking to God. Then I started screaming at him. I didn't fear him because he is my father in every sense of the word and he loves me. That's the kind of love I grew up with from my parents. I grew up with unconditional love and knew that even if I made them mad they would still love me and would never do anything to hurt me, so my rationale was that the same held true for God.

I know that belief about God's unconditional love is valid because all the while I screamed at him and cried that he didn't have the right to take Dad away from me… he let me rant and rave. He's still with me today. And he stayed with our entire family every step of my dad's illness. Through it all, my dad maintained that he would be healed in God's time, not his time. And he was right.

In 2006 Dad received a lung transplant when he had just hours left to live. I had felt that he didn't have long, so naturally when I spoke with him the first time after the surgery, and he sounded just like he always had, I promptly broke down sobbing at my desk. I thought it was all going to be fine from there and I was so relieved that God had healed him, and for a year and a half everything was wonderful. Then he inhaled mold while out walking. After you have a transplant you have no immune system, so this was bad. Everyone thought I was being dramatic when I left his hospital room and was crying, but I honestly thought I'd never see him again. That was in May of 2008. They took my father to the VA hospital in Wisconsin by life flight and I didn't see him again until September of that year.

I had moved back to Ohio in August, and because I was now at a safe traveling distance the doctors felt it would do my dad good to be around family and maybe give him more fight. Honestly, Dad had fought as long as he could, and no matter how much he loved us he just couldn't do battle any longer. The doctors would get a handle on one infection and then find another hidden one. I was losing him again. He went back to Wisconsin in October and came back to my family with my mom in January 2009. I lost my father on February 2nd, 2009 and once again I experienced that overwhelming sense of total devastation.

At the funeral everyone tried to offer comfort by telling me that he was in a better place and I was happy for him, but heartbroken at my own loss. During the service the minister, my uncle, was talking about how Dad was in heaven and they were having a glorious celebration. It was more than I could bear. I doubled over and cried, "I just want my daddy back." That was all I could think at that time. I felt hands on my shoulders holding me and felt peace. I later thought it was my dad, but the truth is I don't think it was; it was God. He was holding me together when I couldn't hold myself together anymore. And eventually I adjusted to the pain of losing someone that was so much a part of me. Not healed, or not yet at any rate; it was too soon.

In April of 2009 I had worked through most of the pain of losing a parent when something new to contend with came along. I was having a hard time walking. My back had been hurting terribly, but I had just attributed it to the scoliosis I had been diagnosed with at age 12. That was what I allowed myself to believe until I'd stand up to walk and my legs wouldn't move so I had to drag my body with a walker to take care of my son. Even worse, I'd be standing and one of the kids would bump into me and I'd fall down. That was when I gave in and went to see a doctor. He ordered an MRI of the spine and found that I not only have scoliosis but five other conditions in my spine. The worst of those is a rare disease called Syringomyelia, which affects only 8 out of 200,000 people. It is a cyst inside the spinal cord that is formed when cerebrospinal fluid is forced inside the spinal cord and does nerve damage. Although my cyst was small, with all the other issues I have in my back, the combination was a bit too much to face. That was when I discovered what my father had meant by healing in God's time. I was so floored by this news that I didn't even know what to think. I was 34 years old and I was disabled. I wasn't allowed to lift anything over 10 pounds. That meant I wasn't allowed to lift laundry, could no longer go grocery shopping alone, and I couldn't even pick up my own child at that point. Standing to cook or do dishes was excruciatingly painful, vacuuming was forbidden, and no matter how strong the pain medication... I was still in pain. I would cry in my sleep from the pain. I did the only thing I knew to do. I prayed to God. I told him that if that was the path he wanted me to walk I would walk it, even if it meant doing it on a cane or a walker. I simply let go because there was nothing else I could do.

For six months I traveled back and forth several times a month to doctors over an hour away from home. I was seen by specialist after specialist... some wanted to do surgery, some ran so many blood tests I was sure I'd have no blood left by the time they were done, but every test came back fine. The conclusion was that my disability was not caused by any one problem, but a combination of many. It was decided the only alternative was to put me into water therapy so that the shock would be less for my back and I might gain a little bit of my functionality back and at least be able to function without a walker.

For 12 weeks I went to therapy 3 times a week and for about 8 of those weeks I would leave therapy so exhausted I could barely make it into the house. I would come home and take the medicine prescribed and sleep because I was too weak to do anything else. Ultimately, day-by-day it became easier... the pain was still there, but I decided to stop the medicine because it wasn't helping with the pain unless you count being knocked out as relief. I may not have been awake for it, but I was still feeling the pain and crying while I slept, so I just stopped taking it. After four more weeks I was finally able to walk without the cane. Physically I was as healed as I will ever be, and walking without the support of either cane or walker.

I don't share these problems with you to elicit sympathy, but rather to demonstrate that you can be hit hard. You can be knocked down to the point you are certain you will never get up because the pain of loss and failure have totally decimated you. That is where I was.

My family was barely making it financially. We didn't have money for the medical bills that were piling up because what my husband earned was just enough to meet the needs of our family. Any credit card bills had to be forgotten, I had to let a car be repossessed because we couldn't afford it any longer, and any added expense was one we couldn't take on. And honestly, we were grateful he was still working with the way the economy had collapsed. Life was hard, but we had a home and we had a family to support. To lighten the load I began looking for work and was quickly disheartened that most of the jobs available to me were barely above minimum wage and were over an hour away from home.

I wasn't in a position to take a job so far from home with three children, no childcare, and only one car, which my husband was driving for his job. Had I opted to take one of those jobs I would have been working to pay for a second car and a daycare provider. That obviously was not the answer. I prayed that God help me find the answer that would allow me to help support our family and still be there for my children. He provided in a way I had not foreseen.

After months of research, in December 2009, I opened List 2 Close Assistant and was able to help support our family while still being home with my children. As a real estate virtual assistant I have been able to pay off debts while working at home. I work in an environment that doesn't cause more damage to an already unstable spine and that for the first time ever is taking us on a path to financial independence. I walk my own path and work – many days I have worked up to 20 hours, because life and business are not for the weak hearted.

Running my own business has been up and down, and I've been through the feast and famine cycle most entrepreneurs go through. I've been in that place of giving so much of myself to others that I honestly wasn't sure I had anything left to give to myself. I've been in that place where I was exhausted, broke, and hated people I was working with, but I kept going anyway. I've knelt before the altar of God and poured out my heart and soul that he replenish me and guide me on this crazy adventure. There, and only there, was I able to find the freedom and clarity my soul had craved.

Through it all, my faith made me realize that tough times can be hard, but it's also where I experienced the most growth. I survived my darkest moments and more; I took the lessons I learned there and applied them to create a life that is filled with purpose, passion, and faith.

I learned to never ask, "Why me?" because I really don't want the answer to that question. It's not about that anyway. It's not about how fast you can get through a difficult moment, week, month, or year, but rather what you learn while in that place. Sure, it's a place to which none of us want to go, but we all have to do it and only when you find your inner strength will you truly flourish and thrive. Mine came from faith that my God does not want me to struggle or be unhappy, but rather happy and productive, and filled with His purpose for my life. He's not punishing me for some unknown wrong. It's never been about what I deserve.

Life and business just aren't about what is deserved, but rather what you are willing to give to those around you. You have to learn to weather the storms, pick yourself up, or even give yourself a good kick in the pants if you want to contribute to this life. If you can't do that you will be little more than an observer in your own life, which gets tossed around with each passing wind. You have to be willing to look past what is and take a step out in absolute faith that there is a higher purpose to the pain you are currently experiencing. And then you just have to do your best to let it go.

Hanging onto past pains and disappointments
is the surest, fastest way to stay in that place in your heart
where life is just too much.

It's a path that leads to broken hearts and dreams, the loss of faith and self. To truly be successful you have to take the knocks but come back for the knockout round. Get mad. Get driven. Get focused. Truthfully, you have to get over yourself. That may seem harsh to you, but not one of us is in this life alone. We are all connected to someone or something. You have to stop focusing on yourself and what you think you need or deserve so that you can step onto the path you are meant to walk. It's a great place when you get there, when you know in your gut you are making a difference to the people around you. And every twist, turn, hurt, and disappointment will take you there. That is what makes you so uniquely gifted to do what you do and makes you the person you are today.

> *For I know the plans I have for you," declares the LORD,*
> *"plans to prosper you and not to harm you,*
> *plans to give you hope and a future.*
> *Jeremiah 29:11*

C3❦80

About the Author

Serita Diana, a former real estate agent with an "on the ground" view of exactly what the life of a busy agent is like, excels at supporting the businesses of real estate professionals and entrepreneurs. She is known as an expert who is extremely talented at creating systems with her clients' businesses and building teams to accommodate her clientele. Believing the marketing plan should be as individual as the real estate agent, Serita specializes in personal strategies for real estate growth. She can be contacted at http://list2closeassistant.com/

CHAPTER 6

Healing Journey

Diane Floerchinger

My challenge in life was my life. I attracted people, circumstances and lack of money as tangible proof my beliefs were accurate. There was always something worse around the corner. Everyone was out to get me.

ଔଓଔଔ

Once I had awakened from the nightmare, I began a healing
journey transforming mind, body and spirit.
Repeatedly stumbling, yet always getting back on the trail.

As a toddler, my mother declared I was intelligent, talented and could accomplish anything I wished. Instead of assimilating those words, I absorbed her dark energy of being a victim. Her negative statements were never-ending. "Out of the frying pan and into the fire;" "Don't trust anyone;" and "We'll (just) get by," echoed at every turn.

Fear froze me in place, left me powerless and swallowed my childhood, and eventually my adult life. The effect of that foundation was evident as soon as school began and games other kids enjoyed felt like physical and emotional torture to me. I quickly became teacher's pet, skipping recess.

I was seven; Mom remarried only to discover her husband was a raging alcoholic who frequented late night bars. When she would wait up for him, his drunken shouting boomed through the wall to steal my sleep.

In addition, I had the issue of poor nutrition to deal with. Mom used food as a sedative to dull the pain of her world gone so wrong and she taught me by example to do the same.

Bullying children turned into cruel teens eager to point out my excessive weight. It only increased the torment that, with the best of intentions, I was dressed in the most unflattering colors and clothing possible for my chubby body. Although I discreetly earned top grades, I avoided doing or saying anything else that might draw attention.

The success of occasional crash diets was short-lived because my inner fat girl was always poised for the first opportunity to take over my body. As soon as attention in any form turned my direction, the discomfort sent me fleeing to a pan of homemade chocolate chip cookies.

At nineteen, I began my first serious relationship with a fugitive from an abusive family. When I failed to support both of us on my phone operator's salary we became homeless. For two years we resorted to living in a car when we could not make our way into no-money-down apartments or motel rooms. The key to the door of any short-term residence was either cunning or money from my boyfriend's sporadic jobs. I was constantly exhausted, and when presented with a bed in any form, I would attempt to sleep my life away. Often, with no other option, I sink-showered in gas station rest rooms; no one guessed I was penniless.

I went without food for days at a time... the feeling of my stomach lining eating itself alive created desperation that left only shreds of my learned morals. I occasionally stole small tips in restaurants in order to buy a can of soup to quell the pain for a day.

Just like a faucet, "lefty-loosey, righty-tighty;" my emotions were shut off at the valve to prevent overflow. I never smiled or laughed unless I was playing a part in the play my life had become. It was us-against-them in great exaggeration, and "we" had to win – or "they" would.

Eventually, my stuffed down emotions began to jack-in-the-box on me. Just like the toy mechanism, they always startled me, popping out at the most inappropriate times. Finally, realizing that my sanity depended on it, I left the relationship.

Having been starved for so long, as soon as I began to eat regular meals the weight began to pile on. Feeling unattractive and unworthy, I proceeded to submerge myself in relationships with sociopaths, drug abusers, alcoholics and many who were so strange that only I could see their magic. I instinctively knew how to *chameleon-ize* myself. Repeatedly, by association, someone had to tell me who I was. My ravenous hunger to be loved and to matter… obscured any glimpse of self-respect and dignity.

There were times I was 'relatively' content – until the next awful thing occurred. Several times I came close to death because of whom I chose to love; other times I simply wished to die.

At size 26, I dropped 100 pounds through real-food nutrition and set in motion a fascination with holistic medicine. I continued to gain and lose the same rebounding 40 pounds. Unfortunately, losing weight did not change my attraction for toxic relationships. When life felt as if it could not get any worse and I could not possibly hate the world or myself more – something snapped! I took the first step in a journey of self-discovery; a daily journal.

I had just been forced into bankruptcy to escape insurmountable debt caused by a boyfriend who had gone under in the current of drug addiction. I vented self-contempt on each page, often gashing the notebook's surface with the pen in my hand. Gradually, my journal transformed into a vehicle of healing. I moved from hating myself... to despising him... to sad acceptance. I tackled my appearance once more by creating a *LookBook* from a stack of notebook-organized photos that reflected my desire for a new image. 'Frumpy' essentially disappeared as visualization took over and 'vibrant' emerged.

Books and the knowledge they contain are treasures to me. Miraculously, I happened upon the classic spiritual book "Creative Visualization," by Shakti Gawain. The words lit me up and literally plastered me against the wall shaking. However, the power of one book wasn't enough to create the entirely new belief system necessary to endure my move from a modern light-filled apartment to a dark dank basement apartment where my husband-to-be lived. I sat in my car each evening when I arrived home, tears blurring my vision, desperately wishing my life would change. Change it did! My desperation installed an invisible "Hit me" sign on my car. I attracted seven accidents in fourteen months; two so serious only fractions of seconds saved my life.

After three years, we moved into a freshly renovated home. In a joyful and curious state of mind, I resumed where I'd left off by consuming mountains of self-help and spirituality-oriented books. It finally became apparent I fabricated my life to be one cataclysm after another!

Further contemplation led to a trail of methods to increase the effectiveness of journaling and reading; many, so common they might be overlooked. Each capable of powerful transformation; books provided the lift to change my thoughts, emotions and circumstances in my life.

I watched movies that made me laugh myself silly, finding it was impossible to simultaneously feel happy and sad, worried and fearful. My sweet cat *boyz* provided a soft blanket of comfort. Their love changed my outlook and provided hope. Music wedged into my heart when often nothing else could; becoming a retreat that transcended dire circumstances.

I generated a project I titled "Soul Resume," to choose my life purpose. I embraced *"Be a light to others by using my enthusiasm to teach, inspire and encourage them to find joy and beauty in their lives."* In the early stages, I interpreted the statement only as being an empathetic manager to staff and clients.

I found my way out of living in my personal jungle... step by cautious step. My negative belief system was so entrenched that I did not always hold my new center. Inconsistency got me at every turn; damp vines of deluded beliefs clung to me. I would progress and they would wrap around me once more, sucking me back in to experience more terror. For years my circumstances fluctuated, depending on how well I adhered to all I should have long known by that time to be true – my thoughts are responsible for my reality!

I was still on a teeter-totter with my weight; feeling alternately fat and miserable and 'less fat' and terrified. It consumed my attention and helped me stay safe and silent. I continued to gauge my value through others' eyes. If they saw me as ugly, flawed, worthless, or inept—then I was all that and more. Being the slowest-of-slow studies, increasing opportunities to get it surfaced. One occasion led to a final crisis point as every part of my life caved in around me and I was mired deep in the jungle once again.

With sudden clarity, I committed to cease being "Drifting Diane." I wrote in my journal and advised all my friends that I would be consistent in thinking thoughts that led me to feel positive emotions as a basis for creating a belief system that would instill a higher energy around me.

I also resolved to pull apart the terror, dissect the fear, and learn to trust myself. The grey haze began to dissipate and better circumstances emerged almost immediately. I watched as my temporarily abandoned Soul Resume unfolded further, with a renewed emphasis on inspiration.

Spiritual metamorphosis commenced with frequent meditation *visits* to the timeless ocean. I developed intuition and began to trust myself as I'd promised. Following sudden inner urgings to delve behind loving lies, I unearthed a profound truth about generational violence that had denied me a father.

I also began choosing my words precisely for effect; I did not 'have to' do anything.

I chose to...

After announcing I was so creative I had to keep a notebook and pen with me twenty four-seven to write down the avalanche of thoughts in my head, I actually had to do just that. When a decision of any type was required, I asked myself if it led me towards the life I wanted to create or away from it.

My Soul Resume unfolded once again; this time *enthusiasm* stood out. A great sense of humor emerged. I concluded I was uncovering my personality, piece by piece... one I'd never had when I was too busy blending into the scenery. With such transformation, I began to look at my body differently. I no longer focused on n o t wanting to be fat; I couldn't focus on the problem and get a solution. I dumped the DIE-t mentality thoughts and files. I opened my dusty 'Look Book' and updated the pages. I learned to accept myself no matter what the scale read. As I established a healthy relationship with my body and food, I stabilized my size at last.

I'd always felt most alive writing. Yet every time I closed in on it, drama came roaring into my life to sidetrack me until I surrendered. When I understood it as just one more way of attempting to stay safe in a dangerous world, I summoned courage to leave the work-a-day world. Following my heart, I founded a business to educate and create inspiration through my words.

I wrote the draft for a book that combined biographical clips-in-time with the methods that completely transformed my life. I also wrote my signature speech on the power of self-talk and set about obtaining speaking opportunities. The victim egg that kept me from my dreams had been shaking and fracturing for some time – when I first began healing my life – I thought I quite simply hated myself. It was shocking to discover that fear and victimization had actually been draining me. At that awareness, the eggshell shattered! I began feeling my way through a new sense of empowerment.

No more "Safe and Silent." I'm living my ultimate "Yes!" life and holding the door open for you to follow. The door exists only in your imagination; fear keeps you from walking through it to a life you can fall in love with.

I believe we are all meant to be lights for one another; inspiration to move forward when we feel stuck, discouraged, or depressed. I would love to think that your journey is made easier because you gain hope, comfort or instruction from mine. Our souls really are Unsinkable!

"Whatever you say after I am…will come looking for you."
- Joel Osteen

ೞೞೞ

About the Author

Diane Floerchinger, an enthusiastic teacher and guide, passionately lives her life walking others through imaginary doors of fear that bar self-empowerment and joy. She spent decades trapped as a silent chameleon in a dangerous world of homelessness, toxic relationships and weight struggles... ultimately to find the courage to escape through a series of metamorphoses leading to mind, body and spirit transformation.

A popular writer and regular contributor to The Village Hearth Magazine, who can be reached at www.holdingthedooropen.com, Diane will be releasing her biography "Journey to "YES!" in 2014.

CHAPTER 7

Make the Hard Times Count

Salenta Fox

At the age of twenty-seven, my eyes opened for the very first time, or so it seemed. I saw my life through new lenses: who I really was and the situation I was in… it was not pretty. Before this awakening, I knew everything in my life was not one hundred percent. I knew there were some very obvious things I was unhappy about, but I did not realize the extent of the problem. Ignorance is bliss, and I had been living in a world of ignorance for a long time.

☙❦❧

I had been living a lie, the lie I told myself to survive.

On the outside everything looked good. I had a beautiful house on the hill, two amazing, smart children, and a husband who provided well for us at a thriving business we built together. That year we grossed over a million dollars after only three years in our industry, which was unprecedented. We had decided to give up most of the pleasures of life, buckle down, and make our business a success. This was the three-year mark, and now according to our plan, we would start to live life. Goals have always been a part of my life, and when I set them, they come true. That cold, snowy Idaho New Year's I made the decision to turn inward and focus on my relationships, my family and me.

The power of intention is a magical thing. Once this decision was made, something bigger than me took over, and a few days later a friend invited us to a two-month life-coaching program. This is where the first inklings of my seemingly perfect life started to unravel.

Let me start at the beginning and give you a little background on how I got to this point in life. I got married three months after my nineteenth birthday. I had only known my husband for five months the day we got married, and half our courtship was spent without communication. I was young; I did what all young Mormon couples do, I got married.

After only a week of marriage, at our second wedding reception in southern Utah, I remember sobbing so hard uncontrollably... the man I thought I knew was suddenly very, very different. But, I was married already, and that was that. I would have to make the best of it; I would have to make it work; that's just what good women did. I was married for time and all eternity, as Mormons believe, and I was stuck here forever.

Shortly after our marriage, I remember driving through the beautiful scenery of southern Utah on the way back from visiting his parents; it was a five-hour car drive back to Cedar City where we attended school. I was divulging my deepest hopes and dreams for life. I wanted to be an herbalist, and practice in the esoteric healing arts. The response I got was very unexpected! I was promptly told and persuaded of the absurdity of such an idea – the argument was that his parents were both educators and would never approve of such a ridiculous notion. I had to continue with my standard university education out of sheer respect for his parents.

His reaction to my life goal took me by surprise and dropped my heart to the ground... this was the man I loved and respected telling me my deepest desires were ridiculous and not pursuable! In that moment of cowering, giving in to what someone else thought was best for me, and succumbing to his judgments, the start of a life unlived began. I gave my power away in that moment. You do this once and it is becomes easier to do it again and again, until one day your soul either seeks to break free into truth and alignment or gives up on life and dies. My soul was headed for death.

It took eight years of marriage in a judgmental, critical environment of belittling and demeaning behavior, and me giving in to keep the peace, for my soul to come to this breaking point. The sad part is, as I made the decision to focus on my relationships that cold December day, I did not know I was even at a breaking point. I was so out of touch with myself, and had given my power away so many times; I was oblivious to everything real around me. This was my coping mechanism.

The man I picked suited me perfectly. I was insecure, I did not feel worthy or adequate, I was very unsure of myself, and I did an excellent job of finding a partner to validate these beliefs every day. It was not his fault I was in this situation... he was just being himself, and my self-concept kept me trapped in an unfulfilled, unlived life.

The first four years of our marriage things went relatively well. But our intimate relationship was always a sore spot and very unfulfilling for me. I wanted intimacy, but the emotionally unavailable man I chose did not want anything to do with it. The harder I tried to remedy the problem, the worse matters got. I bought books... I read them, but he refused.

Four years into the marriage, our daughter had just been born, I remember sitting on my bed and making the conscious decision to just give up, to shut my sexuality down, and forget about even having a fulfilling intimate life. It seemed like the only thing to do to keep me sane. I was shut down emotionally, expressively, and now sexually. I was living a life I thought I should, in order to be the perfect wife and mother, and in doing so denied myself of any real pleasure.

By the end of the course in February, the instructor practically had to hit me over the head to make me see I was in a very controlling and manipulative relationship. I was a millionaire but could spend no money, while my husband spent all the money he wanted to. I literally had to go through an inquisition and fight to spend anything other than bare essentials, and I did not like to fight.

In March my parents enrolled me into another life-mastery training program. I got rudely awakened to the fact that instead of the giving, happy, optimistic person I thought I was, I was really just an empty shell drawing from a dry well. For the first time I saw I was deeply unfulfilled in an emotionally abusive relationship, with the notion if I did more and gave more, ultimately everything would work out. Finally it was impressed upon me I could not give anything to another if I did not give to myself first.

This second training also gave me the courage to speak up and not tolerate the belittling and mean comments directed my way; the same comments I had not allowed myself to hear a few months prior. To finally hear the way my supposedly loving spouse spoke to me was absolutely shocking. I read books to build MY self-confidence, found new friends who supported and encouraged me, and slowly started to see and feel my value.

The more I lovingly did not participate in the manipulation or fall for the emotional abuse, the stronger I got. I realized I did not have to fight to speak my truth, in fact, the opposite was more effective, the more I stayed calm and stood my ground in a firm but loving way the more his tactics failed to work. Not engaging and playing the game freed me from it. My focus was on love; I knew if I always came from a place of love it would be best for both of us.

This time I loved me first. I came to know I could not relinquish my best interest to another. Others, no matter how altruistic, will always have their best interests at heart first, and this is how it should be. If we each always do what is best for us, and come together from this space with love, things work in harmony. Not being selfish, but centered in your truth. As I did this, the more we grew apart with irreconcilable differences. By the end of that year to the day, we were divorced.

The years following my divorce were dedicated to healing and rebuilding. There was a lot of unraveling to do; I was so tightly strung and had to relearn to relax. I started a regular yoga practice, spent as much time as possible outdoors, and started to meditate daily. I found that even though religion did not work for me, I was a very spiritual person. I started to draw on this spirituality daily and realized spirituality is only one of the laws of nature that govern the world, and the more I acted in harmony with these laws the more peace and harmony I found within.

*I took love, and went on a quest to explore it more fully,
to uncover the uncoverable.*

Love became my creed, I wrote about it, interviewed others about it, and dove deep within myself to uncover all I could about this mysterious yet sacred concept. I found it to be the cornerstone of everything… of all joy, pleasure, and peace. The important lesson was that love started within me. The more I loved myself, the more worthy I felt to receive love. I learned that without self-love and adoration I neither would, nor could, allow another to love me.

As I opened to love, the more my soul expanded, and the more I trusted others and me. I realized the things I sought from others were the very things lacking within me. I used this as a guide to heal all the parts I felt I needed from another. I wanted someone to care for me, to love me, to make me feel safe. So I started caring for myself more, creating boundaries to create safety, and did energetic clearing exercises to blast out the unworthiness and inadequacy—replacing it with a deeper self-love than I had ever know possible. I did not think I was unworthy consciously, but the deeper I went, the more I saw my diminished self-worth was at the bottom of all the negative situations I had created in my life.

This realization and clearing changed my life. I no longer accepted behavior and circumstances from others as I had before. My boundaries made me feel strong and safe, and my love grew by the day. I continued the work of going deeper and healing my blocks with intimacy and sexuality. As I opened more into my sexuality I discovered a woman's power lies in her ability to be in her full feminine essence of surrender, allowing, and vulnerability. Without a strong base in self-love however, these concepts were scary; I found them not safe to surrender into. I came to understand why in past history the world tried to block female sexuality and make it wrong and bad. When a woman is bold and confident in her sexuality, she is also bold and confident in life, and cannot be unduly controlled. Her authentic power is directly linked to how comfortable and open she is with her body. This does not mean she sleeps around, it means she is comfortable and at home with all her parts.

In a matter of a few years I had totally transformed my life. That shy, insecure, inadequate girl flowered into an open, confident, loving woman. What got me to this place was a desire to be whole, an openness to get assistance from coaches and healers, and a commitment to lead with love. My darkest road led me to my fullest life living my purpose and sharing my gifts with others. If I could transform in such a powerful way, then I could guide others to transform also.

Love then blossomed into my life mission to guide others to the love within them first, and use that love to lead them to live their purpose and mission also.

"There is a vitality, a life force, an energy, a quickening
that is translated through you into action,
and because there is only one of you in all of time,
this expression is unique....
You have to keep yourself open and aware to the urges
that motivate you."
~Martha Graham

ೞೊಉೞಎ

About the Author

Salenta Fox, Love Consultant and Coach, is an avid speaker, a blogger, and personal coach and consultant working with people to uncover their authentic self, find their purpose in life, and unlock their inner power. A lifelong entrepreneur with a marketing degree from Southern Utah University, Salenta has owned and/or operated multiple successful businesses since her late teens- including a million dollar company. Following an eight-year marriage Salenta – a lover of life and seeker of truth – went on a quest to uncover the power of love. After successfully completing her own journey within, and uncovering her own love, Salenta now guides others to their love and bliss, first within themselves and then with another. This devoted mother of two loves to travel and explore new places in her spare time, and can be found at

http://salentafox.com/.

CHAPTER 8

How Dreams Saved My Life

Dr. Dianne Frost

I must have been born a dreamer, because for as long as I can remember, I have followed the soul's impulse through the language of dreams. As a child, I did not resist bedtime. I actually loved it because I got to enjoy imaginal romps through fascinating realms when I closed my eyes for dreaming. The imaginal also was accessible with eyes open during the daytime when I engaged in theatrical play and creative writing. With my dreamer's temperament, I was always curious about life and often baffled by the way people behaved. My mother wrote an entry about me in her diary that I found after she passed. It said, "Dianne is always so curious about life and human behavior. I think she'll grow up to be a psychologist."

My mother knew who I was in my heart of hearts.

C3ED80

Mothers have a way of knowing that is deeper and more heart-based than typical understandings. She was right about me, even though it took me a great many years to find my way through the twists and turns, storms and smooth sailing of experience, to my soul's dream. I married at the tender age of eighteen, and birthed a beautiful baby girl one day before my twenty-first birthday. She was a gift straight from heaven!

The dream, in which I met my daughter, five months before she was born, has been the most vivid and profound dream of my life. It was more like a super-conscious vision than a sleepy, wispy dream. In the dream, two luminescent angels came to me and said, "Come with us. We want to introduce you to someone."

"Who are you?" I asked. "And where do you want me to go?"

"Don't ask questions. Just follow us," they said.

And so I did. They took me to a void in the middle of nowhere. After a few moments, I saw a golden dome palace, filled with light and joyful singing voices. Out of the palace came a beautiful being. She came towards the two angels and me, and then joined us.

"This is your daughter," the angels said to me. I was awe struck; moved to the deepest part of my heart and soul. The beautiful being was my daughter? She was luminescent and awe inspiring in her soul body. I could see all of her talents and everything about her.

"I am so happy and grateful!" I said to my daughter. "You are more than I ever could have asked for!"

"You are the perfect mother for me!" she said. "I'm very excited to be born! I need to go back to the waiting place now, though. I'll be with you very soon!"

We embraced with great joy, and I felt my heart expand to a thousand times its prior size. How fortunate I was to have such a daughter! She beamed at me with love and excitement, and then she turned and went back to the golden palace. The angels remained. "We want to tell you a little about your daughter," they said. They told me various things about her character and ended by saying, "She is of her father's household, but you and she are spiritual sisters and have a bond that can never be broken."

Whoosh! We fell through space, and I awoke. Wide-awake! Not at all like waking from a typical dream. I woke up my husband to share the amazing visit.

"Wake up. I just met our daughter! She's beautiful!" I said ecstatically.

"Huh? I'm sleeping. Tell me in the morning."

So I let him sleep and sat awake by myself for a long time, amazed and overjoyed. I thank God to this day for the profound dream/vision of that night. I thanked God then for the opportunity to meet my daughter in her soul body. I thank God to this day for that dream/vision because it ended up saving my life.

For the majority of the next ten years, I absolutely loved being a mother and wife. My husband worked to provide an income for our family, and I took care of the household and our beautiful, wise daughter. Our marriage had its problems, but we made it work for the most part. That is until I rocked the boat.

"Honey, I want to go to college," I told my husband.

This deep urge to go to college arose with a passion. My parents were both educators, and I had a strong foundation of intellectual curiosity. I knew in the core of my being that the time had come for me to follow that personal passion, along with my love for homemaking.

63

"No. Your role is to take care of the household," he said. "Our daughter is the gifted and talented one."

"Yes, she is gifted and talented. And I will continue to take care of the household. But I also want to begin college."

"No," he said.

What he did not realize is that I was not exactly asking for permission. My soul's dream was much too strong for me to ignore it. I could not follow my husband's order to stick to my only role as a homemaker. My soul's urge was insistent. It pulled me forward and gave me the courage to enroll and begin classes as a psychology major. Mind you, this was long before I read my mother's diary. She was right. I am natural psychologist.

Stepping into that calling, however, was not an easy journey.

My husband was furious that I enrolled. When dinner was a half hour later than usual because of my class schedule, he yelled at me relentlessly. There was no peace in our home because of my insistence on following my soul's calling. My life felt miserable under my husband's roof. One day it got so bad that I'd had enough. My soul spoke up again.

"I want a divorce," I said.

"Go then!" he yelled. "And take our daughter with you! You and she are close, and I'm busy working. But one day I will take her from you, and you'll be destroyed!"

Escaping from his curses, I did leave, and continued to raise our daughter as a single parent, college-student. A couple years after our separation, however, my ex made good on his threat. He remarried and promptly went to Court. He told the Court that he deserved to be the custodial parent because he was a white, Christian, married father living in a nice suburban neighborhood, but I was a lazy student in a mixed race romantic relationship, living in a ghetto. My attorney told me that I needed to drop my psychology major in college because it took too long to become a psychologist.

"If you want to keep your daughter," she advised, "you need to go for a degree that will convince the Court that you will have a good income soon. What do you like besides psychology?"

"Well, I like writing. I will do whatever it takes to keep my daughter... my heart."

"Good. Then why don't you become an English teacher? English teachers like writing. And you could show the Court that you have an achievable goal."

For the love of my daughter, I switched my major to English. Sadly, that wasn't enough to sway the judge. I was devastated! The Court awarded primary custody to my ex. I had visitation rights, but it wasn't the same. I felt like my heart had been ripped out of me. I cried and cried, ranted and raged. I considered murdering someone – my ex, the judge, someone! But it wouldn't have served my daughter for her mother to be in jail for murder and her father dead, so love for her stopped me. My life felt like it was over. I strongly considered suicide. Without my daughter, I had no joy or purpose. I wanted to die. I was very close to ending it all . . . and then I remembered my inspired dream.

The angels who introduced us had told me in the dream, "She is of her father's household. But you and she are spiritual sisters and have a bond that can never be broken." They knew! The dream was prophetic! She was of her father's household now! And we did have a bond that could not be broken by custody! So I thanked God once again for the beautiful dream, and I released thoughts of suicide. Instead, I visualized a rainbow bridge of love connecting my daughter and me. I held the bridge of love and connection in my heart for the next couple of years, believing fully that the angel's message was true. Within a couple years of our separation, my daughter was back living with me. We didn't go to Court to make it official. She simply said that she wanted it that way, and her father did not resist.

I learned a great deal through my first marriage. I learned to let go of anger, for one. It ate me up at first when my ex gained custody. But after enduring the horrors of what felt like a war being waged within me, I grew fatigued from the pain. It seemed like the anger was a poison that would destroy me if I held onto it any longer. So I let it go. I simply released it and forgave my ex fully. What a relief! Just like that I was free! I knew from the prophetic dream that everything that occurred was predestined, so there was no reason to blame him. Even if there had been a million reasons to blame him, I would have forgiven him. Forgiveness, I discovered, is a powerful balm for healing. I also asked for his forgiveness for all the ways I had hurt him during our marriage.

Although he did not say he forgave me, my soul felt free. I had released all my pain and was free to move forward. The bottom line of what I learned from my first marriage and the temporary separation from my daughter was the immense power of forgiveness, love, faith, and connection. Most importantly, during my first marriage, I learned the power of dreams. The dream/vision of the angels introducing me to my daughter had saved not only my physical life, but also my emotional life. It's a blessing to be able to live without regrets and resentments.

It was in my second marriage that I learned how my soul's dreams had the power to lead me to my deepest calling. My second husband and I enjoyed many years together. Sadly, though, we grew apart over time. We didn't share as much conversation, and our interests grew miles apart, so we rarely shared activities. Even so, we loved each other beneath our differences, so we persevered in our lackluster marriage. I invited him to get counseling with me, but he declined. I really wanted it to work, but it slipped away. A few years before it ended, I was in a lot of physical pain with fibromyalgia and carpal tunnel syndrome. I felt as uncomfortable physically as I felt emotionally. It was partially the lackluster marriage that gave me emotional pain, but it was mostly another kind of discontent. I felt stifled in my role as a public school English teacher. Although I was very successful at teaching and I loved the students, the parameters of State guidelines sucked the vitality out of me. My creative nature could not breathe within the restrictive box of public school expectations. Typical education did not allow me to serve the deeper aspects of soul that I longed to serve in my students. I realize now that my physical pain at that time was a gift. It drove me to investigate solutions for relief. It drove me to discover what was knotted up beneath the surface of my skin.

I began my healing process with the support of massage therapists, who healed my carpal tunnel syndrome. One body worker suggested I see a hypnotherapist for my fibromyalgia. The hypnotherapist was an amazing wise-woman who could see straight into my soul. She not only relieved me of my fibromyalgia, but she helped me to believe in my capacity to live a life aligned with my calling, a life of passion and purpose. I was touched to my core with gratitude and vowed that I would pay it forward someday and do for others what my wise-woman mentor did for me. With her encouragement, I took steps toward my soul's deepest desires.

My soul's calling was all that mattered. I felt pulled. I could not ignore it. I had been physically in pain when I tried to ignore it. I had "no choice," it seemed. Well, of course I had choice. It wasn't the easiest choice, but it was the richest, most fulfilling choice. I was willing to be called back to the dreamer I was born to be and give up living a life of "should." I had awakened to the importance of following a path of soul. During this time I realized that living the life I was destined for was going to take a lot more than just waking up in the morning to live a routine existence. I asked my husband to support me in my soul's desire.

"Sweetheart, I have found a graduate program of Depth Psychology that I resonate with deeply. It is a program focusing on my life-long passions, and I'd love to learn everything about it. I want to discover how to help people to live rich, fulfilling lives. I have inheritance money to cover my tuition and books. Will you support me by allowing me to reduce my teaching assignment to part-time and to contribute less to our monthly expenses?

"Can't you be in the graduate program while continuing to work full-time?" he asked.

"I don't think I could handle it," I answered. "You know that I work around the clock to keep up with grading papers and planning lessons for my 200 students as a full-time English teacher. After teaching all day, I continue to work every evening and most weekends and holidays. If I entered an intense graduate program on top of that, I'd have no time to attend the classes, do the reading, and write papers for the courses. I would so love to teach part-time and enter the program. It's really important to me."

"If it's really important to you, then okay. Go ahead and do it," he answered.

What a kind man he was to support me in my calling! I was elated to enroll in graduate studies for my doctorate in Depth Psychology! Immersed there in a subject that focuses on dreams, soul, and the mysteries of our subconscious mind, I was in heaven. I had found a place that fed my soul's longing and ever-present curiosity about life and why people do what they do. Everything started speeding up. While studying, I continued to teach part-time, I trained with Debbie Ford to be an Integrative Coach Professional, and I saw clients. As if I were not busy enough, I also trained to facilitate Voice Dialogue and became a Board Certified Hypnotherapist. My life was filled with meaning, and it was intense because of doing so much at the same time. I loved going deeper, yet it was challenging.

The biggest challenge came when my husband said he wanted me to stop my studies and go back to work full-time. He was tired of paying more than half of our monthly expenses, and he said he didn't know my doctoral program included time to complete a dissertation following the three years of classes. I was shocked! Having invested a great deal of effort and my inheritance on my doctoral program, and being close to the finish line, I was unwilling to abandon my program and return to full-time teaching.

"I can't quit on my dream now," I said. "I've invested so much, and it means the world to me."

"I think we should divorce," he said.

It hit me really hard, even though we both knew it had been an unspoken undercurrent in our marriage for some years. Now the words had been spoken and the time had arrived. So we separated. Fortunately, we had enough love for each other that we released each other with kindness. No use harboring grudges. I knew already that love and forgiveness are the keys to peace and vitality. It was rough, to say the least, going forward on my own to complete my dissertation. My heart was in shock for a while and my financial stability was nonexistent, yet I continued on my path. There was no turning back.

My soul had taught me long ago that I have a calling that I can go with freely or resist and pay the price. Not being a glutton for pain and anguish, I knew it was best to follow my soul's calling with passion, gratitude, and joy. Looking back, I see that it was important for me to complete my journey alone. My faith, strength, and unique vision were carved more deeply into my being as I journeyed onward. I learned from the loving release of my second marriage that each of us has a path. Sometimes we walk together on the same path, and sometimes the greatest good is for us to walk separately. I also learned that the soul's dreams are the truest compass for living our fullest, most brilliant lives.

While completing my doctoral dissertation on dream work, I learned from my sleeping dreams. One night I dreamed I was crossing an endless desert, heading to the Dead Sea. The dream reflected the scale of the journey I was on. It was a tremendous undertaking. I had invested everything in it, and I was richly rewarded for it. After crossing the finish line of my dissertation and receiving my diploma, I started to have dreams of gold everywhere. From my studies of Carl Jung, I recognized that the images of gold in my dreams were confirming that I had chosen the right path and come into my own true being. In one dream, I was in a store in the Holy Land where I saw raw-gold nuggets. I picked up the largest one and told the store tender, "I'll take this one." I bought the large gold nugget, radiant with light and energy. As I put it in my pocket and walked down the road, I felt the potent light of the gold in my pocket and knew I had something magical, something that felt like source energy, to accompany me on my continued journey.

And the vibrant source energy has accompanied me in my waking life! My life is truly blessed now! I am grateful and deeply happy to be living the dream my soul has called me to live. I can say with all honesty that I would not be truly living if I had not followed the prodding of my soul's dreams. I owe my happiness, success, and very life to dreams! My soul knew from the beginning what path I needed to walk to birth my deepest nature and fully live.

True to my soul's dream, as my mother knew long ago when I was a young child, I am a Depth Psychologist. I coach clients on accessing their inner wealth so they can live the lives of their dreams. I am paying forward the gifts my wise-woman mentor shared with me. I have the privilege and joy of helping other people to tap into their inner riches and find inspiration to improve their lives immensely! I work with business people wanting to access fresh innovations to elevate their business success to a whole new level. I work with artists who want to tap into a wellspring of creative inspiration. I work with spiritually oriented people who want me to guide them to the infinite inner-wisdom that is available to transform our lives from all right to magnificent. I work with people from many other walks of life, as well, and I love them all. Yes, I love them! The dream nugget of vibrant gold in my pocket, you see, reminds me every day that we are beautiful, divine beings having human experiences in our earth-school.

It's the human part that trips us up sometimes and makes us lose touch with our deepest wisdom. It's also the human part that allows us to have learning experiences, even when they are painful and immensely challenging. It is the divine part that rejoices when we do learn, and it is the divine part that whispers in our ears to remind us of who we truly are. I know now that I am not the person in the story I just told. She walked those paths, and she is no more. Like a butterfly emerges from its chrysalis, I am a person in continual process of becoming. Who are you becoming? May you be blessed!

> *"Imagination is more important than knowledge"*
> ~*Albert Einstein*

 conoso

About the Author

Dr. Dianne Frost is acclaimed as a gifted Inner Wealth Coach who has a magic touch for helping her clients to live extraordinarily fulfilling lives. A life-long dreamer who has followed the guidance of her soul through challenging and blissful life experiences, her professional credentials include Ph.D. in Depth Psychology, M.Ed. in Counseling, Credentialed Teacher, Certificated Integrative Coach, and various additional certifications—all useful tools for her passion of supporting people to reach their highest potential. More important than professional credentials, Dr. Dianne is a down-to-earth and openhearted person who uses her intuition and life wisdom to inspire her clients to live abundant, joyful lives. Dr. Dianne who can be reached at

http://www.drdiannefrost.com or http://drdiannejackiefrost.com/

lives in beautiful San Diego, California, where she savors life, writes, and coaches international clients.

CHAPTER 9

The Phoenix Lives Again

Crystal Gifford

The more sharply the bow is pulled back, the farther, sharper, and more forcefully the arrow can fly forward.

Sometimes life just kicks you right in the face, and it is so very difficult to understand the value of the seemingly endless blows while you are in the midst of the trial. Rest assured, my friend, in every trial there is a glorious victory waiting around the corner. My story is one of receiving a big kick in the face again, and again, and again by a life that has led me to more joy than I ever thought I could experience in my life.

Grab your popcorn and let's get started.

☙❧

I started my life… my life, the one I get to create for myself, about seven years ago, following a divorce. I was finally free to create and live the life that I could design however I wanted it. So I set out with hope and a glimmer in my eye for what the future had in store. The only problem... I had no money. In order to support my two boys in the most loving environment possible at the time of divorce, I walked away with almost nothing but a prayer that giving my ex-husband everything would somehow create harmony that my boys would not have to suffer through the usual divorced-parents syndrome of hate and spite. For the most part, it worked, and I am here to say I have been blessed beyond what I could imagine in that process. Within two years after my divorce I had built a six-figure income, my boys and I lived in a house way bigger than we needed, and we were living the life. After struggling through that first year and realizing my boys needed me more than they needed the six-figure lifestyle, I even managed to streamline my work, build up some passive income, and find space in my life for them again. Now, we had the income and the time to really enjoy each other. That was all great for a couple of years, and then I decided I was going to create a business around showing other women how to build the same thing I had built for us. Time and freedom... doesn't everyone want that?

So, I began investing in myself, in the business, and meanwhile in real estate – all to push our dream forward even further. And it went so well for a while; then my resources started to run out. I had not mastered one of the most critical elements of building a business, getting the message out! The marketing piece of my transformation needed some major work and I was quickly sinking financially while I figured this out. After postponing a major event I had spent almost an entire year planning, still owing my team for the work they had put into it, and losing big in a real estate deal, I was seriously at my rock bottom financially... more income than after my divorce, but way deeper into some real financial problems.

Here I was, a wealth mentor with no money! *How does that work for you? Want to come work with a broke wealth mentor?* These are all of the things that were going through my mind. If I had blown it in such a big way, how could I expect to lead others on the path to wealth? My business started to really suffer as my belief in myself, and my ability grew colder and colder. At some point, I honestly considered closing up completely and pressing the quit button, ringing the bell in this business training camp, going back to a simple life where I didn't expect myself to contribute or create so much for everyone. I had the means to do it, and the thought weighed heavily on my mind. I knew mentally I had the capacity to still help others, but my emotional connection was waning fast under a pile of unpaid invoices and failing real estate deals. I felt like a dance teacher who could no longer dance, and I was ready to give it all up. My dream faded into the chaos and I honestly couldn't even hold the vision for the difference I would be making anymore. Worse, I wondered if I even still cared!

What did I do during all of this? I would like to tell you I stood boldly and everything was magically ok. But the truth is, I cried. I cried and cried. I slept in depression, I even found myself cursing God one day at my lowest point. My house had flooded. I crashed my car the same month I had changed it to only liability insurance to save money, and the bank was calling asking how and when we were going to pay on our business loan for real estate. I had taken all I could and I just screamed at the top of my lungs. I was so mad at God and was convinced He was a trickster who showed us hope then stripped it away. I yelled at Him. I cursed at Him, and I told Him to just leave me alone if He was going to keep filling my life with false hopes. I was angry, and I couldn't pretend any longer that I believed it was all going to be ok. So, I yelled at the only one in the Universe I had always trusted to support and save me no matter what.

Once I came back down from my rage, I was a bit nervous, watching for lightening to strike me. Raised in a very strict religion, some remnants of those beliefs were apparently lingering. Plus, I still loved God, just not today. God didn't strike me down; He sure didn't come to my rescue right away, either. I had to learn how to save myself and He was stepping back to give me the space to do it.

I could sense the distance, though I didn't understand why. So I gathered myself, and kept pushing forward after giving myself a few days to pout, spending some time with some positive friends, and looking into what was good about my life. I was almost there. Where? I really didn't know, but somehow in all this darkness I started to think that maybe, just maybe, there was a way for me to be at least ok. I wasn't strong enough to even want fabulous then, but maybe I could be at least ok one day again…?

But that wasn't everything… you see, my youngest son had decided he was going to move in with his dad at 13 years old, and as any mother would be, I was heart-broken and dealing with that loss, and now my 19 year old was going off to the university. I was an empty-nester at 37! Now I began to really understand what depression felt like. At this time, I was still pushing toward a live event where I was going to show all these women how to create financial freedom, something I had done, but I felt like a complete fraud because everything around me had fallen apart over the past eight months. I still pushed because without the event in sight, I felt I had nothing to live for. My boys were gone, my real estate deal was crumbling, my house was huge and empty, my friends were busy, and I lived in a small town with no real social activities to pass my time. The event was all I had to work for, and I was pushing hard at the only dream I believed I had left. The only problem… no one was coming.

I did what any stubborn entrepreneur would do; I took off to Florida in hopes of finding some local attendees for my event since it was scheduled in Tampa. Within one week of being there, it was clear this was not a good plan either, and I just needed more time to fill the event and get myself back together so I could confidently lead the event. *More time? You mean postpone the one thing that has kept me alive this year? You mean let go of the only dream I had left in my sorry little six-figure income broke life?* But what was the point of an event with no attendees? So I took a big breath and pulled the plug.

That was the final blow to my self-esteem, my wallet, and my ego. But in that surrender, once I made the decision to cancel the event, something magical happened. Since I was in Florida, I spent two days on the beach allowing the ocean to cleanse me of all the beliefs and desires I had wrapped around money, success, and the event I was now surrendering. As I lay that Saturday releasing all that I had shrouded around the event, I began to gain a sense of peace like I had never understood before. I released without attachment. I released with relief. I released all that was entangled in my definition of success and accomplishment. That Saturday, I released everything that had ever been programmed in me—or by me and others, who said I had to do anything.

"What if I did nothing ever again to build more wealth?"

I liked the answer that came. Nothing. There was no thunder, no rain, no lightening, no stopping of time, nothing. If I decided to never do another productive thing again, the world would not end. I was amazed, amused, and strikingly calmed at this thought. That day, I released any need to be anything other than me, a human being lying on the beach. Sweet surrender took hold of my previously chaotic thoughts. The idea that I am just as valuable as a human being for being as I am for doing and the powerful sense of love coming from all around me in this beautiful natural scene God had orchestrated just for me that day engulfed me. I was free to just be and allow joy to fill the emptiness that had been so deeply created inside of me from a year's worth of losses. Finally, I understood what it means to be one with the Universe. What a glorious Saturday!

The next day I went back to the beach and again allowed the ocean to blow in its healing energies. This time, I asked the next critical question in my journey,

"What do I really want my life to look like?"

Amazingly, I wanted simple. I wanted love, joy, and peace. I wanted to know my boys know they are loved by me and I wanted to enjoy peace and joy even in the most devastating times. I remind you, my financial situation was still a mess, my boys no longer lived with me, and I was living on two remaining days of Hilton points, which were donated by a friend who knew I was trying to build something and needed to be in Florida. None of my circumstances had changed. So what was different? I was different. I embodied joy. I was finally taking my own medicine and I was finally good enough just for being alive. As I took on all that I wanted that Sunday, I allowed joy in. I allowed peace to flow, and I finally accepted myself for exactly who I **am**, completely unrelated to what I **do**.

The next day as I drove to Orlando for a meeting I had scheduled before I had decided to give up on my dreams, and then found peace beyond all understanding, a true miracle happened. I wanted to cancel, but I decided to make the drive. And there in the sky was a small plane writing something. I couldn't make it out at first, but it soon began to be evident what was being written in the sky for me that day.

Trust!

You see, this entire year as I sought out the counsel of others, as I prayed, as I connected with my own spiritual guides on this journey, when everything seemed to be going wrong, the word that always came was "Trust". I felt a bit put off by the word at some point, wondering how was I supposed to keep on trusting when everything was going wrong. The word had shown up in my life at least 10-12 times in the past three months alone.

Maybe this is a small and seemingly insignificant word for some, but it is the word that let's me know I am supported. And here it was in the sky on a trip for a meeting I almost cancelled, but felt compelled to keep. Trust! It may as well have spelled my name because for me it was confirmation that my decision to stay in Florida was exactly on target with my highest path.

I had decided that weekend to stay in Florida and begin building a life here. I was searching for places to stay and at that point had not decided. Within four days of my decision, I found a room to rent in St. Petersburg. The room was in a big house with several roommates, a far cry from the big house on the hill I was living in at home in Ohio. But there, with only two weeks worth of luggage and a borrowed room with very little privacy, I found myself. I found joy. I found a place on this earth that I could connect to life and disconnect from stuff and accomplishment and pre-defined success. I began to have fun again. I began to feel alive again. And, I was jogging again and finding myself so full of gratitude as I ran by the bay each day that I would sometimes stop and just stare at the beauty that was walking distance from my new home. I met friends quickly, and I found I had so much opportunity that I had to actually carve out work time to stay on task with the work I was still keeping alive. And as you may expect when you get in the flow, I had already purchased a ticket to a live event a couple of months before and it was in St. Petersburg, walking distance from my new home! At that event, I landed a powerful speaking gig and a new program was born that was an obvious cash machine for me, but totally under my radar of perception until one of the coaches at the event pointed it out.

It is called the *6-Figure 2-Hour Workday*. All this time I was trying to do something that I had to build when what I was doing to create a 6-figure income for myself could help the women I wanted to help in such a powerful way! I just hadn't seen it. And here is the best part, it showed up because I had to sit with the coach and vulnerably share the journey I had been on and what was going on in my life. He saw the value in how I earn my 6-figure income and how others could also benefit. Had I not hit rock bottom, this program would have never shown up and those I am helping now would not be able to create the income and time

79

they need to support them in their business ventures. And now, I have the experience of the pitfalls that I can also share to support my clients even further.

It is simply amazing how our darkest moments really do come back around to offer brilliance to our lives. Now I find myself helping others do exactly what I do every day, and this time even a bad real estate deal or a series of unfortunate events cannot erase the work I have done, and continue doing, to change my life and that of others. Now I know exactly how to help others not only create wealth, but also keep that which they have created. Life is truly good.

The lesson I have learned from this journey to the pits of the earth and back is that when we find joy, it doesn't come wrapped in a package. We don't earn it. We could never create it; we simply become it. When we get deep into the space of what we really want, who we want to be, and what it looks like, smells like, and feels like to be that person—nothing else can take it from us. Nothing can give us joy or steal it from our grasp, only enhance what is inside us. Now I reside joyfully in St. Petersburg, Florida and live every day as I wish. I accomplish work sometimes; sometimes I play, and most often I don't really know the difference. Each day is a gift and as my wealth grows once again. I only know that it is simply there to enhance the joy inside of me and to further the difference my story can make in the world. May you be blessed to find your inner joy, for it is there that true wealth resides.

Wealth is the ability to fully experience life
~ Henry David Thoreau

છ૪૦૪ગ

About the Author

Speaker, author, mentor, and seminar leader, Dr. Crystal D. Gifford, known as the Monetization Maven – for her extensive expertise in monetizing her client's message and mission and helping them give meaning to their work – helps others maximize the impact of their success and begin living their dream of luxury lifestyles through financial and emotional development. A visionary leader, with a unique ability to help clients see their own strengths and have the courage to create grand visions for their lives, Dr. Gifford brings the concept of wealth into new light and helps her clients step into True Wealth™. Her philosophy is that money matters should be fun and uplifting, and her approach supports this philosophy; her mantra is "Life is meant to be lived."

CHAPTER 10

Raise Your Vibration

Recapturing Your Lost Dream

Dr. Melissa Hankins

Before I understood how much power I have to create my own reality, I used to give it away in various ways, across all areas of my life: in my relationships, with my work, and even with myself—including whenever I had a dream to experience something different, something bigger, something better in my life.

୧୫୭୬୧

I used to think that other people could actually hold the key as to whether or not my dreams – regardless of what those dream were – could, or couldn't come true. The Divine Universe, whether we call it "God," "Source Energy," "Jehovah," or any number of names we often use to identify This Awesomely Powerful Force, is always supporting us in moving forward. Having dreams and aspirations are all about moving forward and experiencing more in life. The Divine Universe wouldn't give us the power to have dreams and aspirations without giving us the means to achieve them. However, when we struggle with accomplishing those dreams, or when it seems that those dreams are not materializing or aren't materializing "fast enough" in our reality, we have a tendency to want to blame others (i.e., give others our power) for the course our life has or has not taken.

While I have since come to understand that I am a powerful co-creator with the Divine Universe, to create my own reality and to make my dreams come true or not, there was a time when I didn't believe that—when I gave my dream-making (and dream-breaking) power away. If that is something that you've struggled with—giving away your power, or not even realizing you actually have power to give away—and if you've felt like you were losing your dream, then I know where you've been; I know what it feels like to lose your dream and feel dead inside. It's not a completely numb feeling; that would actually be better. No, it's more like being trapped behind three-inch-thick lead glass, covered in a gray film that surrounds you completely.

You see and feel the world from a-far. You may even try to muster up a bit of enthusiasm for something someone does because you remember in the past it made you feel happy. Unfortunately, all that remains is an empty outline of a shadow where that happiness was once experienced. You try to respond in the way you would want to respond, the way you feel you should respond, maybe even the way you once did respond, but you know it's not really you responding… it's your empty shadow-self.

You try to signal to others that you're in distress, that you are in desperate need to keep your dream alive, but then you realize that no one can really help you. After all, how can you describe your dream to someone with as much detail as they would need to find it, catch it, and bring it back to you when the light that once illuminated your dream so brightly that you could taste it, feel it, smell it, breathe it… has now been enveloped in a dark shroud of hopelessness? You stop calling out for help when you realize that no one can really hear you, nor can they see you clearly. People that pass by you may think that you are okay. After all, you're

84

not dead; it's just your dream that's dead, no big deal, right? Get over it, get a new dream, or simply buck up and just get on with life – that's what everyone does, right?

You know, intuitively, that anyone who ever had a dream so real that it no longer was simply a dream, but became their reality... if they experienced that feeling of really knowing a dream deep down in their souls, then they would never say "get over it" or "get a new dream" or "just get on with life." They would know your dream was your life. Unfortunately, some people want to believe that you're okay because they're trapped behind their own lead-glass prison of dreams-gone-dead out of which they have not been able to help themselves, let alone help you out of yours.

Either way, you realize that you are truly on your own – except there is still this tiny voice, this spirit that still resides within you that doesn't accept... won't accept that the dream has died. In truth, it hasn't died; it has just gotten buried very, very deep inside. It's gotten buried underneath layers of doubt, fear, sadness about missed opportunities, questions about your worth and ability, lack of support from family and friends, guilt about taking time and resources to pursue your dream, and countless other things. However, it's still there – its still within you – where you hear its echoes, its whispers. It's fighting to be seen, to breathe... to live.

You begin to have the faintest glimmer of hope; it's muted behind the thick, dirty lead glass surrounding you, but, still, it's hope enough that you begin to think, "What have I got to lose? Trying to live even part of my dream, even if nothing comes of it, is better than going through life in this walking dead state." You start to feel a little stronger, speak with slightly more force, stand a tiny bit straighter. You notice an idea – an idea related to your dream – begins to enter your thoughts, and you start to get a little bit excited —just a little – and a little overwhelmed as you feel some doubts begin to trickle in. Still, you want to take some sort of action on the idea, sure that your glimmer of hope will die again, afraid you'll go back to feeling almost-dead again.

Unfortunately, something delays you once again from taking action in that moment. You try not to get frustrated or scared as the hopelessness tries to take hold once more. You vaguely notice that the inkling of another idea is trying to weave its way into your consciousness. This idea seems a bit more doable at the time, and you accomplish your goal despite finding that some of the same behaviors or obstacles are surfacing and trying to stop you again, but you are determined to push through them—you're fighting for your dream and for your life, and you're not giving up without a fight. You also begin to realize that you're not fighting alone; the Divine Universe is guiding and encouraging you with each and every step along the way, fanning your wisps of hope into something much bigger, much stronger... even though you're still afraid to fully embrace that hope.

I know what it feels like to lose your dream. I also know what it's like to refuse to let that dream die. I know that to let your dream die is to feel dead yourself, trapped in a prison of your own making, a prison resting on fears that are, in truth, not real. A prison lined with regrets about past opportunities not taken, which blind you to the fact that more and often better opportunities surround you and are simply waiting for you to notice and act on them. A prison built by falsely-held self-limiting beliefs about what you are truly capable of accomplishing, having, and being... to fulfill your true purpose in this world while simultaneously living out your dreams.

I eventually realized, as I sat trapped in the prison created by me, by my own mind, that because I had the power to create such a prison, I also had the power to shatter it—bringing it down a crack at a time, or in huge panes of broken of glass, but it would come down! I took it down—with the help and guidance of the Divine Universe—so that my dream, and me along with it, became visible for the whole world to see, to hear, to feel, and by which to be helped.

How do you start to break out of the self-made prison and begin to reclaim your dream? It may seem overwhelming at first glance, but there are a few important points that can make the reclaiming of your dream less daunting, and, yes, actually enjoyable, which is the real key! First, it is important to start where you now are—not where you think you should be, could have been, and would have been, if only…

Yes, it is possible, regardless how long you've been trapped in the prison of fears, limiting beliefs, and regrets, that you find yourself now pretty far off the path that was leading you to your dream. However, there are many more paths open to you as long as you allow yourself to be open to seeing them. These other paths may either be longer or shorter, depending on your ability and willingness to step through fears and limiting beliefs that are still going to arise. The fears and limiting beliefs are simply a part of your human experience and will occur, but they don't have to stop you from doing anything you truly choose to do.

Just think, now you have the benefit of knowing what some of your fears and self-limiting beliefs are because they've already risen to the surface; in truth, you're actually ahead of the game with that knowledge. You are now armed with a sense of what those limiting beliefs are and when they might be triggered to challenge you, and, as a result, you have likely gained the ability to now step through them a bit more easily.

It is important to take responsibility for the role you've played in where you now find yourself—"good" or "bad." You are the co-creators (along with Source) of your own life experience, and by accepting responsibility for the actions you choose to take in your life, you are able to shift from a sense of helplessness to a sense of knowing that you are more in control of your life's path than you may have previously allowed yourself to understand. When you allow yourself to own the outcomes of your life, you realize you truly do have the power to create different outcomes if you're not happy with the current state of things.

Taking responsibility for outcomes in your life also includes the outcomes of relationships with the people in your life, both personally and professionally. When you view yourself as "unworthy" in some way, or "less than," or "not capable," then those feelings become the energetic vibration you are putting out in the world. Therefore, when other people interact with you, particularly over an extended period of time while you are still holding on to and projecting some false belief or low frequency/heavy energy, then that is how those other people will begin to act towards you, even if they didn't do so in the beginning.

You, of course, have the ability to change your "frequency" to one of a higher range, step into your own power, and learn to see and hold yourself as, "worthy," "capable," and "more than enough." When you do this, you'll see that other people will begin to reflect back to you a more positive energy and view of your true, more positively viewed self. Alternatively, if the people around you remain stuck at the lower "frequency," and continue to view you (and, likely, themselves to some degree) in a more negative manner, you also have the power to choose to not be in their company, and, instead, surround yourself with others who see the real you.

Another important point is to not judge or be critical of yourself—it is criticism and judgments (in the form of fears and limiting beliefs) that actually helped create the walls of your emotional prison. Sometimes, though, it can be difficult to take ownership of life's outcomes without being critical of oneself. One suggestion I may offer in taking that responsibility is to acknowledge that you made whatever past decisions or took whatever past actions (including taking "non-action") based on the information and the skills/tools you had awareness of at that given point in time and space. You then say, "Now, that I am aware that I have a different set of tools and skills, as well as having more knowledge about what I truly do and do not desire as outcomes in my life, if I am faced with similar choices again in the future, I will use this newer set of information to make a decision or take an action that is more aligned with what I truly desire to have in my life."

All of that being said, throughout all that you do, it is vital to be kind, gentle, and loving toward yourself. What does this mean? It means to make yourself—not other people or other things—the first priority in your life by taking care of yourself emotionally, physically, mentally, and spiritually, all of which comes down to self-care and self-love. If you aren't loving yourself and investing in yourself, then you actually have far fewer resources (physically, emotionally, energetically) to invest in others, both personally and professionally. Unfortunately, most of us, over the course of our life experiences, have gotten away from our natural state of loving ourselves. It is a state of being that we are born with, but gets buried over time by false self-limiting beliefs that get filtered down to us during our youngest years (from birth through age six or seven years old). Those false beliefs shape our perception of ourselves, including what we "need" to do, be, have, etc., in order to feel worthy of love from not only others, but love from ourselves towards ourselves. It is very important—in fact, it is vital—that we invest in our own self-care, which is an expression of our self-love.

Loving and investing in yourself can take many forms: working out, meditating, journaling, saying daily affirmations, getting a massage, taking a walk, eating healthy, spending time doing things or with people that inspire you, setting clear boundaries with people in your life around creating non-negotiable time just for you, taking a training or working with a coach or mentor with whom you really resonate—these are just a few of the many, many ways you can show yourself that you love YOU.

In summary, the following steps serve as a guide toward achieving self-love:

1) Start from where your currently are, not where you think you should be, and remain open to seeing new paths that could lead you to the dream(s) you have for yourself and your life.

2) Take responsibility for your actions in order to feel more empowered. Know that you are the co-creator of your life experiences, so create the life you truly desire and on purpose, and refuse to live a life by default.

3) Do not judge or be critical of yourself. Understand that the twists and turns in life, the challenges you experience are always opportunities to learn more about yourself, and become the outcomes you truly do want to experience in your life. If you are experiencing an outcome in your life you no longer wish to have, you have the power to change it to create something you truly do desire.

4) Show yourself much self-care and self-love. Invest time and attention in yourself. Some really good ways to do that include journaling, saying daily affirmations, meditating, exercising, healthy eating, and doing activities that inspire you and make you feel happy. Engaging in self-love activities actually allows more of you to "show up" for yourself and for others in your life (personally and professionally) in a way that can actually be energizing and fun, rather than draining and overwhelming.

Ultimately, the more consistently that you engage in positive behaviors, the more empowered you will feel, and the more happiness and joy you will experience in your life. You will also experience increased energy, more creativity, greater clarity, greater abundance, and a more positive outlook on life, in general.

Each step leads you back to not only rediscovering your dream, but you also now having the knowledge that you are the person to make that dream your reality. You may even be surprised to see that as you practice these activities and incorporate them into your life, the prison of your own making, which seemed to hold you back from living your dream has been cracking and breaking along the way, subsequently revealing your dream has already materialized without your having to put so much effort into making it happen!

"When you know yourself, you are empowered.
When you accept yourself, you are invincible."
~Tina Lifford

ೞ೮ಌ೩

About the Author

Melissa Hankins, M.D. is a success and empowerment coach and psychiatrist who helps women to re-connect with their innate Divinely-given power to create a life that is on purpose, creating the life and lifestyle they truly desire and deserve to have, while aiming to reach their highest potential both personally and professionally. Dr. Hankins combines her expertise and knowledge of the mind, body, and various spiritual principles along with her background in executive coaching (in which she holds a certification) to help her clients identify and transform their own self-limiting beliefs and behaviors. She further teaches clients how to replace the self-limiting mindset and behaviors with significantly more empowering beliefs and actions, incorporating these into their lives in order to create a life with greater abundance both personally and professionally. www.MelissaHankins.com

CHAPTER 11

Fat, Black, Broke and Pregnant

La Tanya Hayward

"I am not responsible for anything except that thing in your belly."

These are the words he spoke to me that pierced my heart like a cold steal dagger in the hands of a heartless criminal. This is the man I took the risk to love and who shattered my faith in all men and the world like fine crystal on a concrete floor. Four years I waited for his love to be all my own. I had a rude awakening though as my dreams laid shattered into little broken pieces as he jumped into his truck and drove away. This can't be real, I thought, but quickly realized I had to face the truth about two things: 1) our relationship would never be the same again, and 2) I had decisions to make all on my own about my unborn child. Both of these decisions terrified me as I faced the realization that I would be raising a baby alone. I could certainly feel victimized except I had to be completely honest with myself; I had lived in denial long enough. This is the price you pay when you become involved with a married man. Never, say never, and please don't judge too quickly. If you do, you may find yourself in a situation like mine living a life of regrets. You see, I used to be just like you... quick to judge others, condemning them for things I could never imagine that I would do.

ભ૰ૹ

When I heard gossip about someone else having a secret tryst, my mouth would drop wide open and I would be quick to say, "I would never do such a thing. How could she? How dare he? What a harlot." Then the tables turned around and that so-called harlot ended up being me! Being alone got the best of me... so much that I turned a blind eye to the fact that the man I loved had a wife and two children at home waiting for him after he left my bed. That is no excuse you may say and I do understand your point of view. I used to say the same thing to friends I've known who had this experience before walking a mile in their shoes. After being married to an abusive husband for 12 years, divorced for seven, dating a man who after one year confessed to me he was bi-sexual and another who told me he loved me up until the day he secretly married another woman for her money... oh, and not to mention the one who dumped me during an expensive dinner that I paid for on his birthday, you may easily ascertain that I was definitely looking for love in all the wrong places.

Nevertheless, I kept looking and when I found who I had been searching for I was completely thrown off of my feet. He wasn't what I had expected but because he had a strong interest in Spirituality, I became even more attracted to him because we shared this common interest very strongly. We both grew up in a traditional Christian environment and we both branched out in search of something more to fit what our inner calling was over the years. This was something that was highly unusual for black men especially being that very few even take the lead in the family to go to church. You know what I'm talking about. The black man was either not involved in the church or would bitch and moan about you going; naturally I was intrigued by this man and wanted to know more about him. For me, he was a dream come true but unfortunately, I ignored a very important spiritual principle, "Do unto others as you would have them do unto you."

In the beginning, I avoided him like the plague but then I caved into his advances. I reasoned in my own mind that this must be God's answer to my prayer. We began as friends—a student/teacher relationship—but then our comfort level with one another grew. It didn't take long before the feelings of guilt wore off and we decided we were not going to resist the temptation to be in each other's company more often. He filled a void in my life and certainly told me all of the things I wanted to hear.

He was charming, soft spoken, and a gentleman who filled my head with "I love you's" every chance he got. I could not help but to give him 100% of my love in return. I thought the more I showered him with my love the more I would receive. It wasn't long before I realized that there was only so much of himself that he could give because he had familial obligations to fill. This of course, became really old. Holidays were filled with loneliness and it never felt good to be a secret. Even when we went to a grocery store, he walked way ahead of me rather than beside me to give the impression that we were not a couple.

When we went to special events together and invited to take group pictures, I found myself standing alone on one side of the group, as he would walk to the other side. It was clear that he wanted to make sure that there would not be any impressions of our being together as a couple. More and more I began to feel like a fool allowing myself to be used in this way. There were days

that I would feel so sick inside because of the ugliness that I had allowed myself to be caught up in, but I just did not know how to set myself free without so much emotional pain. As time passed, I had talked myself into believing that he and I should end this madness and be free to be who we are... together. After two years, I became very impatient; I grew tired of going home alone. I became resentful when he mentioned his wife's name. After all, he never wore his wedding ring and he was always telling me that he was not fulfilled in his marriage. When I questioned him about the wedding ring he said he was allergic to it. Who was I to think he would be lying about it? So I continued to believe him, but he never made one move toward divorcing his wife. I dreaded the holidays as they drew near. The loneliness was too much to bear.

There were times I wanted to say, "Enough" but I was committed to him and the thought of not being together was heart wrenching. Day after day, night after night my misery grew. Yet I continued to accept what I was given. I did not have enough self-esteem to believe that I could attract anyone else. It is astounding what you feel about yourself when you have lost sight of your self- worth. My self-esteem had plummeted into the abyss. To support the thoughts I had of myself, the Law of Attraction never failed to deliver that thoughts become things. My thoughts were loaded with venom, especially toward myself. Because I believed I was not worthy of anyone better that was exactly what I got and so I created a very unhealthy lifestyle. Nothing prepared me for the great change that was about to happen in my life.

Back in 1982 my Gynecologist told me, "La Tanya, I am very sorry to tell you this. We have found severe scarring in your uterus that even surgery will not correct. You have a bad case of Endometriosis. You will never get pregnant."

His diagnosis was correct. I never did get pregnant. I was married for 12 years after that diagnosis but could not conceive. So you can imagine how I felt when after all of this time, the unexpected happened. I had never been late, ever, but on that day I was. I took the test and could not believe what it read. I returned to the pharmacy and purchased another test and read the same results. I rushed to my physician, who confirmed I was pregnant. As I sat down feeling confused, I was also very happy but then my joy turned into terror. I had to deliver this news to a man who wasn't mine. I had lived alone for so long and I wanted this to be the best moment of my life. I had always wanted children. I dreamed that someday, I would marry and have three children because I am an only child. With both of my parents gone, grandparents and no siblings, I hated being alone. I did everything in my power throughout my life to avoid being alone and that is why I ended up in the worst relationships because I was so fearful of facing my worst nightmare of being alone. I wasn't willing to wait for the right man to come along. I remember when I was a child, I used to dream of being alone in the night with no one to comfort me, and felt I lived this nightmare every single day until now. At that moment, I sat down and cried hysterically not only because I was happy but also because I was worried about what to do next.

Nothing prepared me for what was about to happen. I had prayed begging prayers all night long before the next morning when I called my partner. When he arrived, I really didn't know what else to do but to come on out with it with no beating around the bush. My heart was beating hard; I could feel it through my chest as he turned the key and let himself in. The moment had arrived and I showed him the EPT. He loves me, I reasoned. I know we are going to be okay. His eyes changed; he looked at me, turned around and walked out. I didn't hear from him for at least three weeks. Needless to say, I was devastated.

When I tried to reach him he'd find an excuse keeping our conversation short. I gave up. He finally did call, but he was angry and accused me of planning the entire thing. Even though he already knew my medical history, he accused me of lying. When our conversations became tense, he'd hang up. Days and weeks would go by, leaving me an emotional wreck. I had no one to turn to. He taught Tai Chi classes weekly so I decided to return to class. After, discovering I was pregnant and with all that was going on I had stayed away but decided to try and get on with my life as usual.

The week I finally returned, I could see the stress in his face and it was very clear that I was the last person he wanted to see. Our mutual friends were happy to see me and had been wondering where I had been because I was never absent. I was his best-kept secret but they all had a feeling we were having an affair.

I knew that they knew but he was in denial. They all knew about his rocky marriage. We were a pretty tightly knit group. Now with the baby coming how could we keep that a secret? The class was near the end so he decided to have us all sit in a circle to share our experiences of the week. I was the last one to share. This was the time I chose to announce my exciting news. "I am going to have a baby." Everyone was excited for me, which healed a lot of my emotional anxiety for the moment. Interestingly, he played along but I knew that was the last thing he wanted me to do. After everyone had left the building all hell broke loose. He was furious with me for revealing the news to his class because he knew they all assumed that he was the father. Our argument quickly became very heated.

We were shouting at each other and then he said something that woke me up in the worst way, he said, "I am not responsible for anything except that thing in your belly." He turned his back on me, walked directly to his van and drove away. I stood there in the middle of the sidewalk stunned. I cried all the way home to my empty apartment and buried my face in my pillows wishing for the sun to never rise again.

After four months, I went to see a doctor who decided to put me on bed rest. He diagnosed me with Pre-eclampsia. I was swollen from head to toe. He said to continue to work would put my baby and me at risk for death. He told me to take a leave of absence and stay off of my feet. I was worried out of my mind. I didn't have any help and didn't know what to do. I had to work to support myself but now I couldn't. Without any financial support, I couldn't pay the rent and my cupboards were empty. I was hungry; being hungry when you are pregnant feels like starvation. I had run out of fuel for my car so I walked to the store nearby in the pouring rain with only enough money to buy a loaf of bread and a package of turkey from the deli. As I approached the store, my eyeglasses slipped off of my nose and hit the pavement. Before I could get to them a car drove right over them and water splashed all over me. I was drenched from head to toe. It was a miserable night. When I returned home, turkey never tasted so good. I managed to live on that bread and turkey for three days. Finally, I swallowed my pride to call him. He came over to offer me $400.00 to have an abortion. When I reached for the money, he sensed that I was not going to follow through and quickly took the money out of my hands, put it back in his pocket and left.

In the future, our conversations were few and far between. I knew it was time for me to make some decisions. The most important decision was to move on with my life. My apartment rent was due. I had received a three-day eviction notice and my electric was due to be disconnected any day now. I was growing more and more desperate by the minute. My anxiety level was over the top. I lay in bed with the curtains drawn day after day and night after night... praying and sleeping was all I could do.

The only sense of joy I felt was when my baby moved in my belly and waking me in the middle of the night, which let me know that we were both still alive. The night before my final day in my apartment a friend called that I had not heard from in six years. When she asked me how I was doing, I collapsed into tears and told her everything. The next day, she came over, helped me pack and moved me into her house in the upstairs bedroom. I will forever be grateful to her. This woman did everything for me, including buying a baby bed and clothes for us.

She was the angel I had been praying for. I continued to live with her until after my baby was born but soon after moved in with another friend. My last move was with a family friend who supported me for at least six months. I could relax for a while but then when his cousins came over to play pool, I became more and more frustrated. Their loud talking and music made it difficult for me to get any rest and would wake up my baby from her naps. One Friday evening, I asked them to please keep their voices down.

Then one of them shouted and said, "Don't get mad at us because you were **fat, black, broke and pregnant.** It's not our fault that you got knocked up. Typical Bi'atch." Every one of them laughed, including the family friend. I went to my room, put my hands in my face and cried. That night, I told God, "If you help me get out of this hell I promise you I will tell the world how you brought me out!"

That prayer became my nightly mantra as I drifted off to sleep. Within one month, I found a job, moved out and started my life over just my little girl and me. When I looked in her eyes each day, this gave me the strength to keep pushing forward. It felt good to finally be on my own again. Life was beginning to feel good, but then depression started settling in because I wasn't getting much sleep. I hated being away from the baby when I had to go to work. I longed for family but no one was there anymore. I didn't have any friends and no one to have an adult conversation with. I only had deep thoughts that were driving me mad. I didn't realize how much of a dark cloud I was carrying around with me.

I only knew my life had changed dramatically with no man in my life to pursue and not having anyone to love. I really didn't know who I was anymore because all I knew how to do was be in a relationship with someone beside myself. Now, things were surfacing that I had buried into an emotional abyss; things that were hard for me to look at. I began to recognize that there was work to be done and this work had nothing to do with my career in health care... but had everything to do with me internally. I had run from me for a very long time, but could not do that anymore.

I began to seriously journal and dig deep into my own psyche and ask myself questions that I didn't have the courage to ask before like: How did I let things get this far? Why did I have this nightmarish relationship? Who am I? What possessed me to have an affair with this man? I learned a valuable lesson and I wrote these words in my journal, "Keep your hands off of another woman's husband, period". This is a lesson I will not have to repeat. I realized that I was filled with self-loathing and that many decisions that I made came from a very dark place inside of me... a place full of pain.

I felt completely broken and someway, somehow, I needed healing on a soul level. After much searching within, I knew that it was time for me to pull all of my broken pieces together and learn to love myself. I finally sat down and took a long look at my life, past and present and recognized just how desperate I had become to subject myself to this kind of emotional torture. I had to learn how to readjust my thinking about the choices I had made in order to overcome all that I had drawn into my life.

Transforming self-loathing to self-love was the most difficult task I had ever undertaken. I never knew how hard it would be until I walked past my bathroom mirror and refused to look at myself. I couldn't even turn on the bathroom light because I was afraid to see myself in the mirror. I felt completely disgusted with myself and with who I had become. I knew then it was time for me to roll up my sleeves and get to work on myself. Even the thought of this was exhausting because I didn't know where to begin and so I decided to stand in front of the mirror, look myself directly in the eyes say just how much I loved myself from the top of my head to the bottom of my feet!

The first day was very hard because I felt like I was lying to myself. I would say the words and then cry in disgust. Many days and nights I would fall to the floor and scream, blaming God for all of my pain. I would say, God, why have you left me? Why did you leave me alone? Through clenched teeth. Why did you take my family away? Why did my mother not have any more children? Why can't I find someone to love me? God, where are you? Why don't you answer my prayers? I was in mental anguish. I felt like I was losing my mind. Nobody knew how hard I suffered. I suffered alone and the next days go to work with a smile on my face. But when I returned home, the pain would rise again as I withdrew into my own world of misery and through this misery trying to heal my anguish.

It was hard to look myself in the eyes.
It was hard to say something

I didn't really mean. Daily, I went through this ritual for about three months saying, "La Tanya, I really love you. I love everything about you. I love your smile. I love your eyes. I love your cheekbones. I continued to tell myself all of the wonderful things I loved about myself until I felt sincere inside about my feelings toward myself. Even when I felt angry and full of self-pity, I worked through those feelings layer by layer saturating myself with love. There were days when I broke down and cried, but I did it anyway because I knew this was about self-preservation. And the fact that I have a little girl who needed me was enough to keep me going. It took several months for me to look at myself again and feel good about being me. One Saturday morning, the sun beamed through the blinds of my bedroom window waking me up and for the first time I felt revived. My self-worth felt re-booted. I learned to appreciate myself and set new boundaries. Above all, I learned how to forgive myself.

Once I forgave myself, I felt free. I re-enrolled in school. I continued to work, take care of my daughter and finally felt good about my life. I continued to write in my journal. I continued to pray and ask God to send me the right man. I wrote a lot of specifics one of which was, God please send me a man that will tell me I will never leave you. One late afternoon I was sitting at my desk in my apartment and my left ring finger had a strange sensation like I had a ring on it but of course nothing was there.

This happened several times. Each time I would grab my finger, shake it and continue to do other things. I was curious about it naturally but didn't give much thought about it. A few weeks later a friend encouraged me to check out dating sites. I was reluctant at first, but then decided to explore a site called Christian Café dotcom. Three days after I signed on, I saw a picture of a man named William. He lived in Maine. I introduced myself and we chatted over the phone a lot. He decided he wanted to meet me. He flew to Dallas. Our meeting was like the Fourth of July. Explosive! What happened next blew my mind. He looked at me after having only been with me for three hours and said, "La Tanya, I will never leave you." Call me crazy if you want, but that day, we were packing all that I owned and I was headed to Maine. I married him July 27, 2003. He legally adopted my daughter as his own and we have been happily married now for ten years.

December 2012 on Christmas morning, I had an epiphany. I wanted my daughter to know her family because she is an only child. I decided to break the cycle of unforgiveness. I recalled how my mother had left my father in California out of anger and because of that I missed out on having a relationship with my family growing up after we moved to Texas. Out of the blue, I picked up the phone and called my daughter's biological father. We talked and shared stories about much that had changed in our lives over the years including our relationship with God. Though we are living separate lives now, with my husband's support, we have come together to build a healthy relationship for the sake of a beautiful child that was brought into this world through the two of us. Since that time she has learned that she has a brother and a sister and aunts who love her. Through it all many lessons about love and forgiveness have been weaved into my consciousness.

The most important lesson has been about self-love. When you learn to love yourself first, everything else falls into place.

"We must learn to live together as brothers
or we will perish together as fools."
Martin Luther King, Jr.

ଔ୫ଓଌ

About the Author

La Tanya earned her Master's Degree in Holistic Ministry through the American Institute of Holistic Theology and her Bachelor's Degree through the International Metaphysical Ministry University Seminary and will soon have a double Doctorate. She is the CEO of Life Navigation Transformation, LLC, a Spiritual Life Coach and Metaphysical Minister. La Tanya's compassion for others motivates her to help people discover how to accept and love themselves. She has dreams of opening her own spiritual center in Maine and is currently writing two forthcoming books, "Finding Power in Powerless Situations" and "Unlocking the Secrets to Your Divine Purpose." You may reach Rev. La Tanya Hayward through her website at

http://lifenavigationtransformation.com or follow her on Twitter: https://twitter.com/LaTanyaHayward

CHAPTER 12

Knocked Down...
But Not Out

Margaret Jackson

My story is one of unbelievable love, excruciating pain and phenomenal strength and fortitude.

I know what it is like to be at your highest, and then at your lowest and be able to come back, conquer your challenges... and rediscover joy.

Being knocked down does not mean that you are knocked out.

C8ꝏ80

In 2010 I found myself in a place where life was really feeling good. I had discovered my true passion and purpose and had made the leap to change careers and start doing what made me happy and what I felt called to do. My career was taking off and I had begun to establish myself in the community. But most importantly, I was honored, proud and blessed to have raised my son, my only child, to be an incredible young man. Richard was everything a mother could hope for... intelligent, kindhearted, selfless and just overall a good person. He was my best friend, a true joy and the love of my life. Life was good.

> *2:00 A.M. —the dog is barking and the doorbell is ringing.*
> *I don't know what is going on,*
> *but I sense that life is about to change.*

With great trepidation I answered the door to two police officers. I could see it coming; I could neither stop it nor get out of the way. I could not run, duck, or hide. The police officers said the words no parent ever wants to hear. They told me that my son had been killed in an accident. *My son was dead.* With one statement, one devastating blow, my world had crashed and I had been knocked down.

I was in a daze. I felt myself losing control emotionally, physically and mentally. I could not say a word. My head was spinning and I was out of breath. I didn't know where I was or what was happening. I ached all over and nothing made sense. The pain was so intense that I had no doubt that I would quickly follow my son. My son, the love of my life, my best friend, and my reason for being was gone.

I had experienced challenges throughout my life, some minor and others more major. Nothing however, had prepared me for this. Nothing had prepared me for losing what I had considered the most important part of my life. I had been blessed with a wonderful child who had become a positive and inspirational young adult. Richard was well on his way to becoming a leader who was as gentle as he was strong. He was both intelligent and humble. He was a person who was extremely kind, and was admired and loved by many. I had looked forward to watching him grow and succeed in life, and like many moms, I had also looked forward to the day he married and had children ready to be spoiled with my love.

But one quick blow... and it seemed that everything was gone. My life, my future as I had imagined it was all gone. I had been knocked down. I was not simply leaning over, or even on my knees. I was all the way down. It has been said that losing a parent is like losing your past, but losing a child is like losing your future. How does one continue... with no future? How does one move forward when there is no future to move toward? Every morning after receiving this unbearable news I awoke thinking there was no way I could possibly continue and make it through another day.

Then one day, in a moment surrounded by the pain and despair of loss, I realized that I had two choices: I could succumb to my agony and give up, or I could choose to survive. I had been knocked down, but I had not been knocked out! I was down and wounded, but I still had a chance. I had spent a good deal of my professional career helping others deal with the challenges of life, and now it was time for me to start to help me.

No matter, how much I wanted to give up, I was not going to let that happen. I could not let that happen. I had to find a way to rise—for me, yes, but also for the love of my life, my son Richard.

Thus began my journey to rise again. My story is about what it takes to get up after being knocked down by life's challenges. My knock down was the death of my child, but the steps I have taken along my journey can apply to anyone having to deal with almost any situation or challenge. The circumstances may be different, but the tenacity and determination needed to survive, are the same.

In our lives, we all have experienced and or will experience situations that are unexpected and perhaps even tragic. They may completely turn us around and knock us down. These situations may change our lives, our direction and even who we are. As a result of these experiences, we may feel as if there is no possible way that we can continue or recover. No way that we can keep going; no way that we can survive. The truth remains, however, that we can recover, and we can survive, and we can find a way to pull ourselves up (no matter how unsteady we may feel). Surviving does not mean that we will be the same, or that our lives will go back to "normal". It simply means that we can find a way back, a way to stand and a way to begin to purposely move forward. We do not have to accept defeat.

Reason to Rise

To deal with challenges, obstacles or even devastation in your life, you must first find a reason to survive. There must be a reason to thrive and a reason to rise above your challenge. Everyone will have personal reasons that motivate and encourage them. Why you begin the journey or steps to rise above life's challenges is uniquely tied to who you are, your situation, and what you want and need in life. Sometimes we may have to think long and hard to come up with a reason that motivates us, and other times the answers come over us like Divine inspiration.

A reason to rise is the first step in standing up
after being knocked down.

For me, the reason was very simple and became very clear. I had to do it for my son, Richard. He was gone, but I needed to keep his spirit alive. I needed to allow as many people as I could to share in his beautiful spirit and in his passion for life. They needed to experience his infectious smile and his desire to fully live his dreams. Richard could not share this with them, but I could. I had to.

And with the desire to rise again came the decision to start RJ Smiles, Inc. This would be a non-profit organization dedicated to sharing smiles and helping people who have experienced setbacks rediscover and achieve their dreams. I could share Richard and at the same time help others. I was now on a mission, a mission that was giving me a reason to rise. In addition, building RJ Smiles gave me an opportunity to pour out all of the love I had to give that no longer had a place to go. And perhaps eventually, it would allow me to smile again.

Having a reason to rise is the first step. It is a step that is crucial to your journey. When you have a reason to rise above the pain of loss, a financial catastrophe, a divorce, an addiction, or whatever your challenge, it allows you to raise your head just enough to get a glimpse of the future and its possibilities. It gives you motivation to go forward.

Lean On Me

As we deal with life's challenges, there are times when it is impossible to rise without the help of others. We may have discovered a reason to rise, and may want to rise, but the load is too much to bear alone.

At this time you must ask for, seek out,
or simply be open to help.

Many years ago, my son invited me to a school concert where he was part of a jazz group. He did not mention anything special about the program, he just asked me to come. Attending his school events was nothing new. It did not matter, if it was sports, music, or an awards assembly, he was always participating in something and I always found a way to be there. On this particular evening I got settled, and began listening to the program. They were a talented group of young people having a good time and performing their hearts out; each song better than the previous. Then, out of the blue Richard and a young lady stepped forward. They began to sing one of the most beautiful versions I had ever heard of my favorite song...

Sometimes in our life,

We all have pain

We all have sorrow...

But, if we are wise

We know that there's

Always tomorrow..

Lean on me, when you're not strong

And I'll be your friend

I'll help you carry on

It won't be long

Before I will need

Somebody to lean on...

Lean on me, Bill Withers (1972)

Richard was singing this song to me and for me, and every word touched me deeply. At the time, I did not exactly grasp why it meant so much... I just thought it was because it was my son singing one of my favorite songs. Little did I know as I intently listened to this beautiful performance, years later I would remember this experience, and need these words, in such a crucial way. I would need to remember and understand that there are times in our lives that are so hard that you must lean on someone.

Helping hands, are all around us.
The question is whether or not we reach for them.

I first reached for an organization called The Compassionate Friends (TCF). This organization was founded by parents who have lost children and is dedicated to helping parents on their journey to healing as they navigate the grief process. The specifics of how the group operates or what is discussed are not important. What is important is that this group was made up of people in

110

varying stages of standing up after the loss of their child. They were people who could share information and experiences and help me on my journey to standing once again. It is important when dealing with any challenge, to connect with people who understand your situation and circumstance; people who can offer guidance as well as empathy.

This group helped tremendously. Little by little I was rising; I was getting up, but the group alone was not enough to keep me standing. I needed more help. I needed to do something I try never to do. I needed to lean on my friends. Asking friends for help was difficult... pretty much impossible. I had grown up helping others, but always finding ways to fix or deal with my personal problems on my own. I needed their help but did not know how to lean on them, or how to ask for help, especially during this time. The solution was not to ask, but to simply allow myself to be open to the help that was offered. This was a small step, but a step I needed to take. Eventually, I took another step and another step. Accepting and asking for help became easier. I was able to lean on others, which allowed me to gradually begin standing on my own.

Standing on Faith

I had come up with a reason to rise and I had learned that it was OK to lean on others and accept their support. I was now standing... but barely. I had managed to rise from life's knock down, and found my ability to move, but I was scared. I had gotten this far but I still hurt too much. Mentally, physically, and emotionally I was still experiencing a pain so deep—being engulfed in so much despair that it seemed like the only thing to do was to take a standing eight count and be called "out". Standing up and actually facing the world, and my future, was hard! Instead of getting easier, some things seemed to be getting more difficult. My experience had taught me to expect this, but I was not ready for it. Now was the time I needed to stand on my faith.

Many of us know that when we have been challenged by the circumstances of life, and have managed to somehow pull ourselves up, remaining upright becomes an even greater struggle. We have expended so much energy getting to this point that we are barely able to maintain. We are up, but capable of collapsing at any moment. We are afraid. Afraid, that we are not strong enough, afraid that around the corner life is going to surprise us with another knock down punch, or just simply afraid of what the future will bring (or not bring).

When you have exhausted all of your resources, and are emotionally, physically and intellectually tapped out, this is when you must reach beyond yourself and those around you; when you move from what you know, to what you feel. Whatever your religious or spiritual beliefs, there comes a time when you must call on something larger than you, larger than your circumstances and larger than your problems. We must connect with a source greater than us, or the challenges we experience.

This is exactly what I had to do. In my case, my faith was that source greater than me, or my challenges. My faith had been with me from the start. I had carried it along as I found a reason to rise and even as I began to lean on others. Now, I needed to let my faith carry me. Every moment I felt myself giving in or giving out... I closed my eyes and asked for strength for fortitude and sometimes even for mercy. I was shaky, but I knew if I wanted to stand strong I needed to remember my reason for rising, accept the need to lean on others and hold tight and stand on my faith. And this is exactly what I did.

Over three years later, I can say that I have risen firmly to my feet. At times I may still get a little shaky or occasionally be thrown off balance, but I am standing strong. I am a fighter. I am moving forward on my journey with determination, perseverance... and a smile. I have a purpose. I am sharing my experiences and helping others who are facing challenges rediscover and find their hope...their dreams...and their joy.

I was knocked down... but I was not knocked out.
~ Margaret Jackson

ೞഅ

About the Author

Margaret E Jackson is an Educator, Speaker and certified Life Coach whose passion is helping women manage change, life challenges, and transformation. In addition to holding a Bachelor's Degree in Sociology and a Master's Degree in Education and Counseling, Margaret credits her life experiences for giving her the knowledge and ability to work with individuals and speak on topics related to overcoming obstacles, facing life's challenges and managing change. Margaret, who can be reached at www.MargaretEJackson.com, is truly a visionary whose philanthropic work, such as founding of RJ Smiles, Inc. touches the lives of many.

CHAPTER 13

Lost and Found

Gina Karr

We hear stories of loss and grief all the time but most people never could imagine it will happen to them. I have heard many tragic stories of loved ones taken too soon, but they were always friends of friends of friends, and then one day it happened to me. And now I am 'the story' told to others. My journey began when my husband Dan was diagnosed with brain cancer in October of 2011. On that day I had to make a choice... to fight with him and keep on living for our boys who were three and five at the time, or let his illness take over our once happy lives.

I chose to live.

ೞ౪౦ಜ

I remember the day of his diagnosis like it was yesterday. It was October 14, 2011 and he went for a sinus scan after being treated for a sinus infection for over a month that wasn't getting any better. When he called me at work from the imaging center to tell me he had to go immediately to the ER and they wouldn't let him drive his own car, I knew it was not good news. My normally short commute turned into two-hours that afternoon. I remember being stuck in traffic screaming, yelling, and crying as if the drivers in front of me had something to do with the oil spill on the highway that backed up traffic that Friday afternoon.

Looking back I realize this was part of the plan or 'the story' that was being created for me. I found out Dan had known what was on the scan but wouldn't tell me over the phone. The traffic that afternoon allowed him the time to process the news before sharing with me, so when I finally arrived and was taken back to him, my husband was at a loss for words.

All Dan could do was shake his head back and forth as in, "No it's not good news." How could he tell me he had two large masses in his brain? He couldn't get the words out so he let the doctors speak for him. We stared at each other for about an hour in disbelief, going back and forth mentally sharing our questions, *Why him, why us, why now? Why would this happen to a good person?* He was so young and healthy, and had two little boys that needed their daddy. It was truly a surreal, out of body moment. The rest of the night was a whirlwind. Dan requested I take over and make all the decisions going forward. Thankfully he married a very strong independent woman who was up for the task.

Dan was given a life expectancy of 15 months at the time. Our happy, chaotic life came to a halt that October as over the next 11 months Dan underwent two brain surgeries, radiation therapy, chemotherapy, 10 hospital stays, inpatient and outpatient rehab, countless doctors' visits, lots of setbacks and medical problems, and ultimately loss of motor skills which put him in a wheelchair. Our beautiful, happy home turned into our own private hospital complete with a hospital bed and all the special items one needs when they are immobile and dying. And all of this was happening while I was taking care of two little boys and working a full time job. I was his nurse, his wife, his support

116

system, his best friend, his punching bag, and his rock. I endured more in those 11 months than I ever imagined one person could go through in a lifetime. The demands and sacrifices often led me to sink to the floor in tears, deeply sad, and guilt-ridden over the difficult choices I had to make.

My family, friends, and the most amazing medical team from Johns Hopkins and Gilchrest Hospice Care surrounded me with their loving support, but I still felt alone in this nightmare that was my new life. Part of the turmoil was because Dan and I shared everything and never had any secrets but I had a big secret I was keeping from him – he was dying.

That may sound crazy but with the position of his brain tumors, he was unable to process the reality of his diagnosis. While that may have been truly a blessing for him, it was excruciatingly painful for me. I couldn't say goodbye, I couldn't tie up loose ends with his help, I couldn't talk about anything that referred to dying. I had to pretend as if he was going to get better, defy the odds, and get back to work because that is what he believed!

Dan's illness progressed and got much worse by August and at that point, my sweet husband just laid in his hospital bed, in my bedroom, sleeping up to 18 hours a day, not eating, and barely communicating with me. And on September 13, 2012 he was gone. I remember going to bed in the wee hours as I always did, not knowing if that was his last night with me or not. Dan's hospital bed was next to our bed so I was used to not sleeping. He was unconscious but I still spoke to him as if he was his normal self. His breathing was so heavy and labored we knew the end was very near. My mom slept with me that night; she knew it was time and didn't want me to be alone. It was around 3:00 AM when we both woke because it was silent. Yes, we were wakened by the peacefulness of the room. I opened my eyes and could see my mom over him, touching his heart to see if he was still breathing.

We turned on the lights and kept checking and checking his pulse. Although we knew he was gone, I think we were both in denial. Then she left the room so I could be alone with him one last time. I don't think the events of that night will ever fade from my memory.

At the age of 43, I became a widow with two little boys. The unwanted designation of widow was hard earned. My life was changed forever and although the path that led me to widowhood wasn't very long, it brought a lifetime of pain. A few months later while spending time putting the pieces of my life back together; I was laid off from my job. Instead of going to a dark place having two losses back to back, I held my head high and continued showing my boys that we would keep on living. They knew daddy was gone and never coming back, but were too young to understand the deepness of my pain and the energy it took for me to wake up and go on each day. I had no choice but to do it for them.

They were my why... my purpose.

The grieving process really is a roller coaster of emotions. I know during the first year some of my feelings included fear, guilt, sorrow, courage... and feeling happy, sad, relaxed, crazy, tired, energetic, devastated, content, elated, weak, grateful, strong, and loved... just to name a few.

Grief disrupts our lives in so many ways. We each handle grief in our own way. Some people withdraw, some cry publicly, some hide their grief and cry in private, and some of us just keep busy and never slow down because when we do it hurts.... a lot. I am the kind that keeps busy, but it's how I best cope. I am aware I took the busy route because I didn't want to even notice that everyone else settled back into normal routines while my routine

was empty. I didn't want to focus on how to fill that empty space so I filled it the best way I knew how – being busy and moving forward. Notice I did not say moving on, I said moving forward. People often mistake these two actions and here is how I like to look at them.

Moving forward means remembering Dan, while finding a new direction in life, looking for meaning, and taking it one second, one minute, one day at a time. It does not mean a loss of the years of memories, the relationship, or the love we shared for each other and our boys. It also does not mean Dan will ever be replaced. The hole in my heart will remain, but my heart is growing and open for more.

And what I found when I opened my mind and my heart six months after I lost Dan was that I am still me. I realized that even though I now don the title of widow, it doesn't mean I stop doing all the things I love. I am still the same person who enjoys the same things. I may have lost Dan, but I did not lose my identity. I realized that it is okay to enjoy my life and do what makes me happy.

I know firsthand that losing a spouse is one of the most stressful events a person can experience. The feeling of not belonging anymore is devastating, because most young widows don't have a single friend their age who knows what they are going through, making it even more difficult to find yourself again after the loss. Unfortunately, grief doesn't come with an instruction manual to provide us with the right or wrong way to grieve. We all own our grief journey. Grief is not something that should be compared and there is no timeline. Everyone bounces back from loss differently and that is not a measurement on how much we loved our spouse. So I stopped wondering what I did to deserve this new life, and I embraced what I did have and what I love most, which includes writing, traveling, parenting, running, and my newly found spirituality.

All of these things have truly helped me find myself again and given me a new purpose. I now step outside my comfort zone on a regular basis and push myself to limits I never knew possible. One of my biggest passions is now running. It allowed me to set goals and give me something to strive for that wasn't about my kids. Training for races became my own personal therapy sessions. Crying on long runs became cathartic for me.

I live my life out loud. I made a choice to live for the moment. Live life to the fullest. Some days I get busy and they are still tough, but at the end of the day I make a conscious effort to never take a moment or day for granted because it may not be there tomorrow. My spiritual journey has showed me that there truly are no such things as coincidences.

> *The last year of living without Dan has made me*
> *truly believe with every fiber of my being that he is*
> *guiding me from the spirit world.*

In the last year I have learned that one never gets over the loss of a loved one but time does make it immensely better. I have learned so much about human nature and a new perspective on how people handle grief. My memories have transformed from those that elicit tears to those that trigger smiles and laughter—sometimes at the same time. I now love very deeply. And in a very strange way, I feel blessed. I do not wish my story of sadness and pain on anyone, but I do wish my perspective on life to all my friends.

So it's true that everyone has a story. But we don't create our own stories. I believe our stories are a culmination of events that happen to us while we are busy living our normal lives. We can control what we do with the story we've been given, but we can't go back and change the events. If it were that easy, we would all be living the dream now wouldn't we? Learning to find ways in which to honor your loved one's memory while moving forward in a healthy, life-affirming way, is the ultimate key to bouncing back.

Hardships often prepare ordinary people for
an extraordinary destiny.
~ C.S. Lewis

ଔଓଓ

About the Author

Gina Karr is a mom, a sister, an aunt, a professional, a story teller, a blogger (although lapsed many times), a Christian, a runner, and an ordinary person , passionate about inspiring others to live their best life no matter what cards they have been dealt. After losing her husband to brain cancer in September of 2012, Gina turned her grief into good by running for charity to support brain tumor awareness and the Johns Hopkins Sidney Kimmel Cancer Center where her husband was treated while fighting his illness. She also survived her own grief by sharing with other widows how you can truly live a full life after loss by embracing your passions and utilizing them as a tool on this very personal grief journey. Gina lives in Maryland with her two sons Carson (6) and Tyler (4).

http://notimeforgrief.com

CHAPTER 14

Reality is the Leading Cause of Stress

Nancy Kay

The doctor's receptionist handed me a clipboard and a pen and I sat down to start filling out the forms. Reason for today's visit: to get the widespread redness removed from my face so that I could look better for job interviews in this crazy, competitive job market where any slight thing can kick you out of the running.

But the real reason was that I had been crying
every single day for more than a year.

ೞഏൟഏ

Now it was time to rise like the Phoenix from the ashes and try to measure up to those who achieve success in the work world, no matter what has been going on in their personal lives. At age 45, I was going through a complicated divorce and trying desperately to find a decent paying full time position with benefits, after 20 years of being out of the workforce... while raising three children who are each five years apart in age. During my years out of the job market, I shouldered the vast majority of parenting responsibilities for all three children since my husband was required to travel three weeks of each month for business reasons and our family relocated every two to three years to advance his corporate career in sales.

Investing in my husband's career advancement, no matter what sacrifices were necessary, was something we had mutually agreed on together to benefit our entire family financially over the long term. My husband had started at the bottom of a large company at the time we got married and his perfectionistic, workaholic ways had helped to move him up the corporate ladder one rung at a time during the last two decades.

He agreed to any job transfer at any time—if it would help to move up the crowded corporate food chain and improve our family finances. As a consequence, we ended up buying and selling seven different homes, moving all five of us to various states throughout the country, and most of the responsibilities that came along with each of these stress-inducing family relocations fell squarely onto... me!

But that way of living came to an abrupt halt when the large transportation company he worked for was taken over in a surprise merger. Suddenly, it didn't matter that the van lines still had our family's furniture weight in their computer system. We ended up having to move yet again, but at our own expense so that my husband could take a two-year contract position with a start-up company. Job security and anticipating future financial gains ahead had quickly become a thing of the past.

> *Can you remember a specific time in your life*
> *when suddenly everything changed?*

For me it was during a typical morning routine of making up our king-sized bed during the week of Thanksgiving in 2006.

While tugging to stretch the shrunken cotton sheets to fit over the corners of our king-sized mattress, I just happened to glance behind the bed and noticed that the phone line to the phone that I had always kept next to my bedside for safety had been unplugged from the wall outlet behind the bed.

Curious about what that could mean, I headed downstairs to the kitchen to check out the answering machine there. I noticed that it was currently not turned on, a pattern that I had recently become aware of during the past week. Realizing that it was apparent that someone had been trying to call me, I started dialing back all the numbers on the Caller I. D. to find out who it could be.

That was when everything changed.

The man I was talking to, whom I had never met in person, said he had been trying to reach me by phone for several weeks to let me know that his wife had been involved in an affair with my husband for quite some time. He went on to explain that he and his wife had recently gotten into an argument and following that argument he had locked her out. His wife then moved into a place that my husband had rented so the two of them could be together. As the caller described the approximate location; I was stunned to find out that it was just a few miles from our marital home.

Despite my life-long belief that divorce is wrong, I now had to figure out how to navigate through the fast approaching black storm in which I had found myself caught. Despite my numbness and severe state of shock, I knew that finding a highly skilled attorney and figuring out how to pay for legal services was essential. Besides the tremendous fears I was experiencing, I also wanted to minimize the impact this cataclysmic disruption would cause our three children.

Time was of the essence when it came to hiring an attorney since my husband had previously filed for divorce five years earlier with no advance notice to me. Back then, I had opened my front door and was served with a divorce complaint from his attorney that included a financial restraining order, which forbid me from using any of our joint credit cards. Although my husband had gone on to cancel that divorce action the day after I had been served, I never forgot how quickly he could limit my means to pay for anything.

The very next morning after I got all three kids on their buses, I asked my neighbor to come over to help me start calling family law attorneys out of the phone book. I sat next to her crying, having no idea what to ask each time my neighbor handed me the phone. Dreading each phone call I made as I kept trying to find a family law attorney to speak to who wasn't at court, I thought, *Why isn't there someone to call that specializes in wives who are falling apart due to their husbands having a huge mid-life crisis and completely going off the deep end? Someone with strong knowledge about the legal sides of divorce and custody disputes, yet who also has a deep personal understanding about the devastation that comes from being abruptly discarded?*

The next 18 months were filled with a blur of affidavits, financial subpoenas, depositions, expert witnesses and a trial that got cancelled at the very last minute when the magistrate went out for lunch that day and without any prior notice, never came back that afternoon. After the forensic accountant, children's therapist and court-appointed guardian ad litem attorney for the children left the courthouse that day along with both of our personal attorneys, I realized firsthand just how many highly paid experts make their financial livings off the bread and butter from providing reports and expert testimonies in chaotic, contested divorce cases.

By the summer of 2008, my legal tsunami finally wrapped up when our attorneys spent several days hammering out the contentious details that led to a final settlement. Although I received the majority of parenting time after our parenting skills had been thoroughly assessed, I also was now expected to earn my own living and provide financially for our children as well. All this after having had my career opportunities diminished as I supported those of my spouse!

During the divorce process, my husband's attorney had required I meet with a vocational assessment expert who reviewed my 20 year old college degree in journalism I had earned before our marriage, and then had the audacity to ask me about my current skills to determine what I would be capable of earning. When I explained to him that I had been out of the job market due to my husband's constant job travel and our frequent moves, plus the need for flexibility to parent our third child who had a chronic health condition since birth and a significant learning disability... this so-called expert coldly explained to me that there was no way to calculate all that in numbers to add to his written report. The vocational expert's not-so-fully written report was then submitted to the court by my husband's attorney so the magistrate could use it as a basis to impute the amount of income I was expected to be able to earn.

While going through the legal process, I decided to enroll in an intensive one year paralegal program through a law school which I hoped would provide the education I needed to land a job. As I was finishing up the last of the required classes for my paralegal certificate during the fall of 2008, major banks in the U.S. began to crash, like dominos... one quickly following another. As the economy headed into a free-fall, the job market tightened up and the attorney who had previously offered to hire me when I graduated abruptly rescinded a paralegal position I had lined up during the summer.

I was ineligible for unemployment insurance to fall back on since I had been out of the workforce for so many years. Although I eventually received some spousal support, I needed it to pay for the tuition I owed from my law school paralegal program and pay

127

the extensive legal fees I was responsible for from the lengthy contested divorce and custody battle I had gone through.

Financially, I was stuck. As the residential parent for school placement purposes in the parenting plan, I was required to continuously live within the expensive suburban area in Columbus, Ohio that surrounded my children's public schools and live in specific neighborhoods that aligned with each of their bus routes. Moving back to live near my parents and brothers in Denver, Colorado for emotional and practical support was not an option either, since Ohio is a state that considers a parental relocation to be a significant factor for modifying custody arrangements.

As 2008 turned into 2009, I became increasing frustrated with the fact that the hundreds of carefully targeted resumes I sent out ended up in the black hole of some unidentified person's email inbox. *Was anyone bothering to take even a 30-second glance at my resume? Were any job applicants actually getting hired for any of these online jobs I had been applying for daily?*

I checked in with some of my classmates from the paralegal program I attended and learned the cold, upsetting truth. None of them had been able to get hired either, except for a select few who were hired to represent the big banks' interests as the banks dealt with a record number of homes in foreclosure that were winding their way through the legal process. I also discovered that the bigger law firms in Columbus had let their younger attorneys go en-masse, and these hungry young attorneys then applied for the same paralegal jobs that I was trying to land.

After going on more than 70 job interviews during the next two years, the only jobs I was offered were for short term office positions that included micro-managing, verbally abusive attorneys, endless hours of sitting in a cubicle typing tedious government forms, and a long commute to the downtown area with no paid parking, since most attorneys preferred to work close to the downtown courthouse.

Despite hiring three different job coaches, drafting several resume renovations, enrolling in computer skills classes at a community college and joining a weekly job networking group, I still couldn't find a permanent full time job. I scanned online job sites several times a day and applied on Craigslist so often that by now, even my golden retriever could submit my personalized cover letter and resume.

It wasn't supposed to be this way!

I had played by the baby boomer rules... going first to my own state university and then attending the rest of college out of state to earn my bachelor's degree from a highly regarded journalism program. After moving back in with my parents for a brief time, I married my college boyfriend and we started planning our lives together.

Even though my mother had been a stay-at- home mom, she had raised me, her only daughter, to firmly believe that it was possible to have it all and so I should go out now and take on the world. Her well-read copies of Gloria Steinem's MS. Magazine were scattered all over our house. Bring home the bacon, and fry it up in a pan. Have several well-enriched children and raise them with solid values, the love of the arts and good grammar. Mom had taken me to the public library each week for as long as I could remember. She herself loved to read history books, memoirs and biographies. She taught me that reading about how real people deal with challenges and overcome obstacles is so much more meaningful than reading fiction. What she wasn't able to teach me was how to successfully manage a fledgling career in TV news, a husband with an extremely demanding corporate work schedule and raising kids all at the same time... without drowning in the chaos.

Despite completing several internships in radio and TV news during college, including a rigorous daily unpaid internship as a production assistant at the ABC news station in Denver during my summer break, I discovered after graduating in the mid-eighties that it was not possible to get hired in Denver where I had grown up since it was considered a major news market. After learning that I would have to start out working in very small media markets and continue to zig-zag around the country for quite a few years, I was very discouraged and worried about safety and how to manage living on my own wherever I could find an entry level job.

I felt so misled by the parental rule book which said that earning a college degree along with several outstanding recommendation letters would be the ticket to an exciting career in television where I could then work and live in the city of my birth. That was when I changed my direction and decided to pursue motherhood. My colicky firstborn had me up at night for years and I longed for an uninterrupted stretch of sleep like others yearned to get a month long paid vacation. After discovering the extremely high cost of quality daycare and dealing with my husband's new assignment to the night shift and his travel schedule, I put my resume away.

Twenty years and several kids later, I found my own true path. I started my own divorce and co-parenting coaching business, dedicated to guiding others from all over the U.S. who are navigating through the storm of divorce that cuts across all the many parts of a person's life.

"Life can only be understood backwards;
but it must be lived forwards."
~ Soren Kierkegaard

જ૮૭૬૦

About the Author

Divorce Strategist and Co-Parenting Coach, Nancy Kay, provides strategic guidance and support through the challenges of separation, divorce and co-parenting. Combining her family law paralegal experience and coaching skills she shows you how to navigate through divorce and co-parenting and get the outcome you deserve. Writing about the pain, frustration and breakthroughs accompanying divorce and being an expert contributor to Huffington Post, "Life Thru Divorce and Divorced Moms," Nancy Kay can be reached at

http://movingforwardthroughdivorce.com

CHAPTER 15

From Broken To Brilliant with Self-Care

My Transformational Story

Elena Lipson

Like many of us, I've learned the hard way that self-care is a non-negotiable and essential element of my life as a mother, wife and entrepreneur. I've also learned that self-care rituals do not need to take months, weeks or even hours. As a mama and business owner, there are many demands on my time. Some days it can seem impossible to take time out for myself.

છ૪૦૪

Yet I also know deeply that self-care comes from planting the seeds of self-love and self-worth. When taking care of your body becomes a transactional idea, as in, *"If I take good care of you and give you what you need, then you will give me what I need,"* you can lose the true connection of giving to yourself in a way that honors the deep rooted understanding that you and I are each part of this divine world. When you connect to that most divine aspect of yourself, then you begin to take care of your body, mind and spirit in a way that is not based on a passing mood or any other external factor. This is when the transformation happens; this is when the mindset of self-care becomes divine inspiration.

For me, it took the loss of all I knew in my life and the diagnosis of pre-cancerous cells to shake me up and change life, as I knew it. Even though I have always known how important it is to take care of myself, I found that knowing the importance wasn't enough... I was unintentionally neglecting parts of myself that would prove to be very painful. Personally, this neglect hit me hard in 2010. As I sat on the floor of my bedroom sobbing, I couldn't pinpoint the exact problem or emotion I was feeling, but I knew something had to change.

I know depression. Throughout my teen years, I was mostly a happy, positive and social kind of girl. But I had a few bouts of deep, dark depression. These episodes of depression were certainly no surprise. My parents divorced, my father had remarried and started a new family, and I ended a long-term relationship all within a few short months. That's the kind of stuff that turns your world upside down and forces change upon you. Even when my father died suddenly of a stroke, the sadness came and I processed my grief.

I've always known how to get myself out of that kind of depression. By exercising, talking about it, journaling, and getting out into nature, I could process my emotions in a healthy way. But this time, as I sat sobbing on the floor in the winter of 2010, I knew that this was unlike any depression I had gone through before. I could feel the darkness of the hole I slipped into and I wasn't sure how to get out of it. On the surface of my life, everything looked wonderful. I was in a loving supportive relationship with my husband, I had a sweet, happy and healthy child, I had supportive friends, and yet I was feeling depleted and shattered on so many levels and in a way that I had never experienced before.

On the inside I felt a darkness descending upon me up. And on top of that, I felt guilty about feeling so sad and broken. I no longer had a grip on myself. It was as if I was losing a part of me and I didn't know how to deal with it. I was angry, frustrated, sad and exhausted all at the same time. I had the sense that everything that I knew about myself and who I thought I would become had shifted just out of reach.

And on top of that, I didn't really want that life back. I was stuck in a place of no longer being who I was, but not yet who I wanted to be or was becoming. While I felt alone in my dark moments, I also had this deep sense that I was going through something profoundly transformational. I felt that I was going through something that other women had gone through for ages. I had the sense that I would emerge at some point. I just couldn't quite see the light yet.

Physically, my body was off balance and reflected my inner world in a big way. Although my diet was healthy, I had painful monthly yeast infections, terrible bend-over-in-pain PMS, a sharp mystery pain in my abdomen that sent me on a journey of CAT-scans, ultra-sounds, colonoscopies, elimination diets, psychotherapy, endless blood tests and the discovery of fibroids, cysts and pre-cancerous polyps that would have eventually developed into colon cancer. This was a journey I didn't expect at such an early age. I was scared.

Ultimately, not one doctor or expert had an answer for me that made any logical sense. They didn't know what was happening to me, or why my body was breaking down so suddenly. They suggested medication, even anti-depressants. I was told by one doctor that "Maybe your uterus or ovaries are just very sensitive to pain." *Uh... yeah right! That must be it!*

(*Sarcasm, of course*). I knew there had to be another way to get out of this place of deep dark shadows.

My saving grace showed up in the form of a five-month "Psychology of Yoga" intensive class that my yoga studio was offering. I felt called to do this program. My husband knew how bad things were getting for me physically and emotionally. He felt like he was living with a different person from the one he had married. We agreed that we would invest a large chunk of money in this program, which felt scary as hell. After all, I was not working a full-time job with a steady income. I was just beginning to figure out how to balance starting a new career with my life as a mama and wife.

Once the yoga intensive program started, I committed to following the schedule and assignments. Through the lectures and weekend intensives I was able to dive deeply into my patterns, habits and my life purpose. I learned all about physical anatomy and spiritual practices within yoga that have continue as daily practices in my life to this day. Looking back now, I can see clearly that while learning about anatomy and spirituality were extremely valuable and important in getting my health back on track, it truly wasn't either of these things that created the life-changing paradigm-shift in my mind.

The real shift began because I was investing in myself in a big way. I was telling the world around me that I was worth it. I was asking for—and taking—non-negotiable time for me, above all else. By learning how to ask for what I need in all areas of my life, I began planting the seeds of confidence, courage and commitment.

The first time I took an entire Saturday away from my family to spend the day doing yoga I felt a deep pang of guilt in the pit of my stomach. After all, there was cooking to do, boo-boos to kiss, a husband to connect with and laundry to fold. And yet, as I sat in that gorgeous, turquoise, incense-filled space surrounded by a circle of beautiful women, knee to knee, I felt an opening in my heart. I felt a melting of something that was unspoken. I felt myself giving my inner-heart permission to take deep soulful care of my mind, body and spirit. As I sat surrounded by my new tribe, I cried tears of release and joy. I cried and opened up to this new space I was creating.

This was not a pedicure, manicure, and monthly massage sort-of self-care philosophy and mindset. This was a deeply profound putting-myself-first shift in perspective. You know that old flight attendant speech that you sleep through at the start of every flight? The one where they tell you to put your oxygen mask on first, and then help others? I logically understood the reasoning behind it before... but I can now feel the wisdom of that now in a whole new way. By shining the light on me first, I give myself permission to be authentic, loving and abundant in my own life. And by doing so, I inspire others around me to do the same. Through this transformational time, I learned that I am the foundation of my life, my family and my business.

Today, creating a daily rhythm and ritual of self-care has become an unbendable cornerstone in my life. I know that the journey of transformation will continue and I am excited to expand into my life and open my arms to receive all the abundance that is coming my way.

And then the day came when the risk to remain tight in a bud
was greater than the risks it took to bloom.
~ Anais Nin

CROSO

About the Author

Elena Lipson calls herself a kick-ass Self-Care Mentor & Strategist, through whose programs, courses and retreats she works with budding women entrepreneurs , teaching them how to take care of their most important asset: Themselves! Her training is extensive, having completed CoachU's Personal and Corporate Coach Training, Executive and Group Coach Training with Trilogy Coaching Institute, Yoga Intensive Teacher Training at Red Mountain Yoga Institute of Yoga Psychology, and is a Certified Life Coach with Coachville. Elena's passion is helping women tune-in to the wisdom of your mind, body & spirit starting now; her premise is "Taking time to care for yourself is not a guilty pleasure. It's the key to thriving in life and business.

CHAPTER 16

Make a Choice for Positive Change

We Are All Given Choices

Jayne Rios

Every choice we make affects the outcome of all our tomorrows. Every move we make is a result of a choice we made. Choices and outcomes are the result of what we are thinking; what we think is a choice we make. The choices you make today will affect your outcome for tomorrow, good or bad.

೦೮೮೦೮೦

We are all given choices in life. We have a choice to continue what we are doing and receive the same results. We have the choice to be defeated; we have the choice to triumph. We have a choice to be grateful; we have a choice to complain. It's the everyday choices we make in life that determine our next steps. Create a vision for yourself and choose to take each day one at a time, making daily, good choices that will impact your life.

Make one good decision today that will
determine your path for tomorrow.

Wow, I wish I would have known that 20 years ago! It's taken a long time to learn those lessons. But I have learned them—as my Grandmother would say "You've come a long way baby". I could go into detail about my life story and the many sorrows and challenges I had to face as a child, teenager and young adult; suffice it to say it wasn't the best. What hurt me most, looking back, was my attitude about what was going around me and ultimately the horrible choices I made. My excuse was to escape my issues instead of reaching out and learning from others and being more open minded to change.

Rosebud

My nickname was Rosebud growing up. My mom called me that almost every day. I used to love it until I was 35 and realized I was actually just now becoming a blooming rose. Honestly, I really should have been a blooming rose in my 20's! Instead, I found myself in my mid 30's, and just realizing my full potential and what I was intended to be... a loving, caring, thoughtful person with strength, dignity and a bright future in front of me.

How the choices I made in life would have been so much better if I had only known this before. You see a Rosebud is beautiful, but it's closed. It hides inside itself for protection and shelter; it's comfortable in there. When its petals are not exposed, the storm does not wither it. It doesn't and can't reach out to anyone for help because it doesn't know how to open and be exposed. Trust is a very difficult thing to do for the Rosebud. If it doesn't open, it thinks it is safe.

The truth is the Rosebud wants to open because that is what it was made to do, but it doesn't know which petal to open first. If it exposes one petal will it need to expose it all? Will there be other roses out there like it? Can it protect itself from the storm if exposed?

These are a lot of issues I related to as a 'Rosebud.' My head told me that no one was going through or had to experience what I had. I saw one crowd and thought, *I am not as good as they are, and they won't understand me.* I saw my girlfriends had really great family lives and I could see the difference... always feeling the need to compare my life to theirs. Of course they loved me for me, but not until I was a 'Blooming Rose' did I realize that. I felt less than other people, and it was a bad feeling. And of course my head played along... I would stop myself before I started, I would second guess myself in everything I did, I let others opinions sway me left then right, I was a people pleaser, always looking out for the other person but neglecting myself. This went on for over 20 years. Needless to say the choices I was making were not of sound mind.

The other day a friend and I were talking—she knows I am writing about Choices in Life—and we were talking about a situation I was in resulting from a choice I made 17 years ago and she noted, "Well, it's the choice you made!" I responded, "Yes but that choice was a result of my environment, not being of sound mind, and not being capable of making "good, positive" choices for myself." So now I had the choice to end the trauma and turmoil, or make the best of it. I chose to turn it around and make the best of it, knowing I still have a choice. No matter what age, you have a choice.

The Rosebud must take life day-by-day, moment-by-moment. Each petal must open and begin feeling its worth. Day by day it makes the choice to get up, move and open itself to the elements of this world. Each day it gets more strength to open more petals and trust more. Every new element is a precious gift and valuable lesson. Raindrops become its best friend... in those storms the Rosebud learns its greatest lessons and receives more strength. In the sunshine it learns to feel joy, love, peace and hope. It strives each day to become a fully developed Blooming Rose.

Blooming Rose

A 'Blooming Rose,' which I proudly call myself today, is open and free and feel's beautiful on the inside and is not afraid to show off. It's open to the outside air, sunshine and all of the weather elements. The Blooming Rose has learned that nobody's life is perfect and it's okay to make mistakes. It's open and honest about its life and every petal is a precious trophy. Every petal is unique and with every raindrop is a valuable lesson. The Blooming Rose knows its value and realizes every day is a precious moment, so it enjoys itself; dancing in the wind and sending out sweet fragrance for all who come near.

What I have learned working with my clients is that no matter your age you can become a 'Blooming Rose.' It starts with believing in yourself, connecting with the right people, and learning the secret to turning off negativity in your head and switching to positive thoughts. Blooming Roses know the power within themselves and aren't afraid to show it. It took me 20 years to learn these lessons; the following tips will help you follow my journey... from Rosebud to Blooming Rose.

> I located really good self-healing books ("Breaking Free" by Beth Moore is excellent). I never went the 'counselor' route, but for some this is a really good option. Ask yourself if you would benefit from the services of a Christian Counselor.
>
> I forgave everyone who I thought had hurt me, intentionally or not.
>
> I wrote down the goals I wanted for my life, not based on past, current environment or whatever else. I embraced what I wanted for my life... the dream I had as a child, or the new dreams I had for a better future.
>
> Given my current situation, I wrote down the steps it would take and the choices I would have to make to have that life and achieve my dreams. (I say "given situation" because you may

have to get up and move to get out from where you are and achieve the life you want. It is sometimes easier said than done.)

If you are in a situation you know is not right for you, please start an action plan to move forward and make the right choice for you, not anyone else. Only you know what's best for you and until now you may not have realized that you have a choice.

I began to visualize myself living that dream life and every day I made small choices that moved me closer to my goals and dreams.

I began reading the Bible about who God says I am, and found that as very powerful and empowering!

I stopped listening to the negative thoughts in my head. Some people put rubber bands around their wrists and when they begin thinking a negative thought they pop themselves, I am not suggesting this... but whatever works!

It took almost one whole year for me to finally master shifting my negative thinking. Now, whenever I get less than beneficial thoughts, I am quick to respond and switch my thought process to positive reflections. This is an important step to control self-doubt, which only you can master. Ask God for help, read the Word, it's full of positive reinforcement and will remind you of who you really are!

I opened my heart to being grateful for everything in life. Because of my open heart, my trip to Africa was life changing. If you are bitter or jealous or think life is unfair, take a trip to a third world country and you will begin to count your many blessings.

The choices we make every day affect our life tomorrow, 10 days from now and even 10 years from now. If we choose to remain positive, forgive our trespassers, trust one another, love mankind and cherish those every day moments, our lives can be transformed into a place of rest, peace, joy and hope. Make a choice for positive change today and watch your life flourish!

"Peace I leave with you; my peace I give to you; not as the world gives do I give to you.
Do not let your heart be troubled, nor let it be fearful."
John 14:27

ೞ൙ൟ

About the Author

Jayne Rios, CEO and Founder of three companies, and an Intellectual Property e-learning system, has 25 years' experience in TV and marketing. Author of *The Interactive Author: Monetize Your Message* and co-author of *Networking to Increase Your Net Worth, {An} Unsinkable Soul* and *Change Your World,* Jayne is passionate about helping others achieve the quality success she has earned. An entrepreneurial spirit with a heart for serving, Jayne is the wife of a prime time, major market TV Director, and the mother of two young boys… filling out her life as a cub-scout leader, a baseball coach and a life skills coach for teens.

Jayne can be reached at jayne@expressyourselfelearning.com.

www.expressyourselfelearning.com

www.lovemeansforever.com

CHAPTER 17

We Don't Do That in Church

Lynn Schreiner

It was the early 1970's and I was an eight-year old little girl, sitting in the hard wooden pew of the First Baptist church where my parents were married a decade before. Our young family didn't attend church very often, so it was an unfamiliar place to me. I didn't have any understanding of why we came to church, or what the meaning of it all was.

☙❦❧

During this rare Sunday visit, I recall being very bored and easily distracted. I was just trying to pass the time until the torture was over. As the minister was preaching, I reached into my little girl purse, took out my little girl comb and began to run it through my beautiful long chestnut brown hair. I loved my long hair with short bangs, and I felt pretty when it looked pretty.

It wasn't long before the elderly church lady sitting behind me tapped me on the shoulder and said in a condescending tone of voice "Young lady, we do not comb our hair in church!" Embarrassed and humiliated, I wanted to leave that horrible place and never return.

Except for attending on Easter or Christmas, our family never did become regular churchgoers and I was perfectly happy with that. As far as I was concerned, God and church were for others. Others... like the popular recording artists you saw on television accepting awards for hit records. They would always thank God first in their acceptance speeches. I always thought they were just being "showy."

During my sleep over visits at her house, my grandmother Mamie taught me *The Lord's Prayer.* I was happy to memorize it and prove to her that I could recite it back, but the words had no meaning to me. I was just a little girl and the scriptures were too hard for me to understand. It would be decades before it would all make sense, and I'd realize what she was trying to impart into me as a child.

During high school, I had two best girlfriends who I spent most of my free time with. Both were required to attend Wednesday evening religious classes at the Catholic Church their families belonged to. They hated the religious classes, and each week would complain about having to go, which made me grateful my parents were not the religious type. I was free – or so I believed.

I can't recall anyone in my family openly talking about God or spirituality, so I had no idea anything was missing from my life. My life was normal, as far as I understood it to be. Like many young women who are spiritually lost, I spent my early adult years seeking happiness in relationships with men, and material things. My happiness was fleeting and I never felt whole or complete. While searching for happiness and a love that wouldn't leave me, I gave away many pieces of my soul.

I was well liked and had many good friends and people who truly loved me. However, I could never seem to shake off the feeling of loneliness and longing. It was as if something outside of myself eluded me. I was reminded of a children's learning toy that is shaped like a sphere with many sides to it, and has many shapes cut from it: one for a square, triangle, circle, moon, rectangle, cross, star, oval etc. The small child fits the matching shaped block into the corresponding hole. When the right block fits into the right shaped hole, the piece falls into the center of the sphere. Obviously, my life was like that many-sided sphere. It was well rounded, with family, friends and many interests.

However, there was one "spiritual hole" in me that was God-shaped, but I'd spent my entire life trying to fill it with people and things. As much as I tried, none of them ever fit perfectly and I remained very frustrated and lonely. At twenty-seven I was still single and I'd been through a series of difficult relationships that left me full of shame, and confusion. I had been used and beaten down inside my soul.

Mike and I had been friends for years, and our friendship blossomed into a relationship that led to marriage. Together we were raising two beautiful little girls. We lived in a suburban household, had two dogs and a swing set in the back yard. I was physically in good shape and took good care of myself. I was an entrepreneur and owned a successful nail salon. Yet... something was still missing!

Sadly, my beliefs and thinking back then were mainly focused on getting more and having more... not becoming more. I was so empty and incomplete on the inside that I believed I'd simply married the wrong guy. Daily, I wrestled with feelings of being a bad mother. No matter how hard I tried, the unhappiness kept following me year after year. I found myself feeling I wasn't good enough, and that my life just wasn't important. I couldn't seem to keep the house organized and clean, and I felt like a failure. I didn't want to tell anyone, so I chose to internalize my feelings and pretend everything was ok.

The day I physically tossed a bowl of Cheerios with milk clear across the kitchen, I knew my emotions had hit rock bottom. My three-year old daughter was fussing over her breakfast cereal, and I snapped. In my outrage I threw the cereal as a release. My daughter was frightened by my outburst, and it brought her to tears. Already convinced I was a horrible Mom, I now had evidence to prove it!

> *Who throws a bowl of cereal clear across the room?*
> *What was wrong with me? I had waited so long to become a*
> *mother, so why was I failing my little girls?*

These were my own self-imposed questions. I cleaned up the cereal mess, and then I let this episode of "coming unglued" haunt me.

Seven years into our marriage, I was feeling very distant in my relationship with my husband, and I felt it was best for everyone if we divorced. I made the sacrifice and choice to allow my girls to remain with their father in our family household and I moved to an apartment nearby. Mike was more nurturing than me, and that frustrated me. At the same time, I was very grateful he was such a great father. I knew they would be safe with him.

In my heart I knew I wasn't leaving my girls, I was allowing their loving Papa to be the custodial parent so I could find healing and become the Mom they always deserved. I reasoned that I was only going to be a mile away, and he'd agreed to allow me to have them whenever I wanted. It was the right choice for us at the time, yet one I have second-guessed and cried over many times since.

> *In my determination to be unsinkable,*
> *my fifteen-year journey to healing began...*

I moved into a tiny apartment close by. I was busy unpacking and setting up home, when the news on television reported the untimely death of the beloved Princess Diana of Wales. I remember how saddened I was about losing Diana. In some small ways our lives were paralleled. Diana had two children and was about the same age as me. Diana was beautiful on the outside, but seemed so torn on the inside. The world knew of her struggles; they were plastered all over the media. I would have been horrified if the world knew my personal story! I was full of guilt and shame.

Newly single again, I jumped right into another relationship. This time with a man who would change the course of my life in a way I couldn't imagine. I easily fell in love, and yet again was dependent on a man to make me happy. After two years of dating, Richard surprised me and ended our relationship. Late one Saturday night, after a four-hour conversation that lasted into the wee hours of the morning he said, "Lynn, I can't make you happy. Find God and you'll truly find the happiness you have been seeking for so long." That was the last thing he said before he hung up the phone, and broke my heart into a million pieces.

I cried all night, feeling like my life had just ended. In reality, it was just beginning, I just wasn't aware of it yet! The next day, and each Sunday that followed I visited many local churches in my effort to find God, and new happiness. The churches were pleasant, but nothing moved me. I was alone and miserable with my thoughts.

About two months after our break up, Christmas day was approaching and I anticipated it would be a day full of loneliness and gloom. In my effort to be distracted and just get through the day, I made plans to spend most of my day with another single friend, Michelle. We'd been friends for years, and while she was a little quirky, she was fun to hang out with. Having spent Christmas Eve with me, my daughters would be going with their father early in the morning. Michelle and I planned to share breakfast at my apartment then go to see a matinee movie.

When Michelle called at the last minute and asked if she could bring along her friend Bill, a Christian friend from the gym, I reluctantly agreed. She'd mentioned Bill previously, and had described him as a nice guy and very comfortable to be around... "Sort of like an old leather shoe" were her exact words. I expected a geeky looking guy carrying a bible under his arm.

Michelle had become a Christian about six months before, and her new life style had driven away many of the single friends we had hung out with. Once a party girl, she now spoke of God in almost every conversation. It was too much. She had given away her television set to focus more time on reading her bible and had "Dress for God" notes taped on her closet doors. Sundays were God's day, and she wouldn't wear makeup and there would be no primping. She was completely in love with God, and it was weird. I was curious, but not ready to transform my life in that manner. If knowing God meant I'd be expected to behave this way, I'd have to say, "No thanks!" I liked doing my hair and wearing makeup on Sundays!

It had snowed recently and the sun was shining brightly that Christmas morning. When the doorbell rang, I questioned if I was really up for this "Double Christian" encounter. I just assumed that all Christians acted like Michelle, so it would be two against one. Expecting the worst, I opened the front door. Standing before me was a muscular, tall and tan, good-looking guy with a huge white smile and no bible under his arm. Hmmm, maybe all Christians aren't the same I thought. Bill shared that he, too, was recently divorced, and had two daughters the same age as my girls. We chatted all morning and throughout the movie, and by mid-afternoon when he left to pick up his daughters, I was convinced that this was the best Christmas present ever. Suddenly, my life looked more promising!

The next day, Bill invited me to join him at his church on Sunday. It was just a mile from my house, and I'd driven past the building many times, yet I always thought it was for "the others". I was, however, more interested in seeing him again, so I accepted his invitation. I was so moved by the church atmosphere and the hope in the message the Pastor preached that something inside of me stirred. Jesus was the God-shaped piece that I'd been missing all my life, and the answer to what I'd been searching for since I was little. I accepted the gift of eternal salvation, and accepted Christ into my heart that day.

As a new Christian, I expected to see and feel an immediate and significant change in my life, but I didn't. God didn't just wipe away all my pain, struggles, fears and frustrations like I pleaded with him to do. My negative thoughts and feelings were allowed to remain as He worked in and through me, to help me emerge a new and healthier woman. I learned to trust God, knowing he would work all things together for good. Even the moments I felt as if I was sinking, I ultimately knew I was healing and he loved me. Still, there was a continuous battle going on in my mind: the old me verse the new me. The old me would win on many days. I was making slow and steady progress, and some days were becoming a lot easier than others.

Bill and I were a couple for about three years and I desperately wanted us to get married. I couldn't imagine life without him. I was in turmoil because my daughters didn't care for him. I knew God had said "not him" when I prayed about our relationship. Yet again, I had repeated my old pattern and it was uncovered. Bill told me that he felt I was putting too much pressure on him to make me happy, and he ended our relationship.

Lord, how did I end up here again?
Why do I keep repeating this cycle?

I spent the next year alone, and searching for answers. I poured myself into spending time alone with God, reading and surrounding myself with positive uplifting people. My pastor consoled me saying, "Someday this pain will be behind you, God will reveal his plan, and we will rejoice together." I had grown to trust my pastor, and felt he knew God much better than I, so I could trust him.

I really wanted to be a good mom, and to be at peace with my thoughts and myself. I was tired of this struggle that was going on inside my head. That year off was the best gift I could have given myself. It was the first time in my adult life that I was truly single and not searching for love from another person.

When I felt whole and able to be happy without being in a relationship, I knew I was ready to date again. In 2005 I met my husband, David, on Match.com and the same pastor rejoiced with me the day he married us. As I write this, we've just celebrated our eighth anniversary. This marriage has been an interesting journey, with its own ups and downs but this time I have approached it with a new mindset. I'm no longer allowing my happiness to be dictated by my circumstances.

On this transformational journey called life, I've learned that there is no such thing as a perfect partner. Perfection lives only in our beliefs. When we believe that the other person should act a certain way, and then they don't, we have set ourselves up for disappointment. Our mindset is made up of our beliefs, attitude and actions. I spent the majority of my life believing that my true happiness could only be found in a relationship. I didn't realize that being happy was a choice I could make no matter what my circumstances were.

During my sabbatical from dating, I was reading a book and came across nine words that would change how I approached life. "Change your thoughts, and you can change your world". Now that was an interesting concept!

I can change my thoughts?

Sounds funny now, but back then I didn't realize the power that God had given me to change anything I was thinking. I just went about my days, thinking by default, running my conscious thoughts through the filter of my existing beliefs and reacting to my life instead of responding to it.

In my business life, during the past 26 years I've had two very successful careers as a nail salon owner and a Realtor. My personal and professional lives are all one as far as I'm concerned, and many of my clients have become friends. I believe in being authentic in everything I do, and letting people see the real me.

During the past decade, I've sensed that God was going to stretch me even further, in a bigger way, so I could help even more people. Three years ago it became clear to me that my natural gift of encouragement matched with my personal struggles, had qualified me to coach others on how to adjust their mindset, and live with more Faith. I'm now a professionally certified and God qualified coach for women of faith. I love helping women discover God in the daily moments, embrace their inner desires and stretch themselves even further so they can live to their truest potential while here on earth!

If you feel like you're sinking today, know that God is there to save you. Let him do his work in and through you, and you'll begin to realize just how much he loves you! God uses our varying relationships like different grits of sandpaper, to smooth out the rough parts in us. Some days He's using the heavy grit sandpaper it seems – but the result will please you!

If you feel like you are sinking, here are some valuable lessons I've learned that may help you!

1) Look back on your life, and realize that moment-by-moment you have made it to this moment. Therefore, what you have needed in the moment has always shown up. All there is IS this moment. Each moment will lead you to the next, and each answer will show up exactly when you need it.

2) Understand that thoughts are not real, until we make them so. A thought is just a thought, unless you AGREE with it. It's when you agree with it that it takes on life. You are creating your life, based on what you are thinking. God gave you free will, and made you able to reject any thought. He hopes you will dwell upon the truth of what he says about you, and his promises found in the Bible.

3) Never allow yourself to be the "Lone Ranger". Being the Lone Ranger is a huge danger! Tell someone else what's going on. It's keeping things to yourself that can lead you to being in a desperate place. Find a friend to talk with and share what's going on inside. God created us to live life together. He made it so we'd need each other.

4) Pray and ask God to put new supportive friends into your life. He will.

5) If you haven't already done so, find a good church family and a place to belong. It will do your soul wonders to learn about God, and have the opportunity to know Christ on a deeper more intimate level.

6) Get a coach who you feel comfortable with, and invest in yourself! A coach can help you see what you can't already see, and empower you. The answers are already within you dear one! Sometimes you just need a bit of help to bringing them forth.

7) Open your heart, and accept that no matter where you are today, God can and will take you to a whole new level if you'll invite him to!

8) Take personal responsibility for your own life. Choose your own thoughts and actions. Do not hang onto the past and blame your parents, siblings or others for whatever your journey has been. God has allowed some things to test you, and your experience is what has qualified you to now help others who might be going through a similar situation. Today is a brand new day and you have the power within you to create a new script for your life!

"Change your thoughts, and you can change your world".
~Norman Vincent Peale

ೞೞೞ

About the Author

Lynn Schreiner, founder of Think on Purpose, LLC, is a woman in pursuit of God and her calling is an International coaching practice, focused on helping women of faith from around the world, get to their next level of joy and success.

Growing up, Lynn did not know God or realize she could have a loving relationship with him. She wandered aimlessly through life searching for her true happiness in men and material things, while seeking constant approval from others. Determined to win her heart, God ironically used two of these men to lead her to church and to him. Lynn made some serious choices that left her questioning herself. God redeemed it all and has taken Lynn to a much higher level of faith, awareness, success and joy.

Now in her "Fabulous 50's", Lynn transparently and joyfully shares the lessons that her journey to mid-life taught her and how they have really deepened her faith and transformed her life for the better. She want's the same for you! She's available for Private In-Person Coaching, Skype Coaching, and VIP Private Intensive Days, and can be found at www.FabulousFaith.com where she's hopeful to connect with and inspire you!

CHAPTER 18

Seeking and Finding Miracles

Karen Sebastian

Miracles happen every day—we just don't see them. When you get the "call" that changes your life forever, it's like time stands still and you slow down enough to appreciate the events that make that day memorable and miraculous.

 ⊰⊱⊰⊱

It's been almost a year ago that I got that call. I was searching through old Facebook messages and saw one I sent my husband a little over a year ago. I was telling him that my phone wouldn't charge and so I needed to communicate through other means. I was conducting training classes in another state. I had a very early class that morning. I usually ask everyone to turn their cell phones to silent but I didn't worry about mine because it was not working. Imagine my surprise when my phone rang. I noticed that it was my daughter and returned to the training class. I set the group up with an activity and walked out of the room so I could call her back.

"Hi sweetie, what's up? I asked casually. "By some miracle my phone just decided to start working."

"Mom, Dad died last night!" she said abruptly and then started sobbing.

I felt like I had been punched in the stomach. I found a chair so I could sit down as I struggled to process what was happening. The last two and half years had been tough on my husband as he struggled with Muscular Dystrophy. He could not swallow so we fed him through a feeding tube in his stomach. He spent a major portion of his day suctioning his own saliva. His diaphragm had stopped working so he depended on a respirator to regulate his breathing. Just the week before his pulmonologist had encouraged him to go ahead and get a tracheostomy as he was not getting enough oxygen through the facemask. My husband wrote "NO – thank you!" on his white board.

As we drove home from the doctor's office that day I asked him why he wouldn't agree to get the "trăch." He could not talk due to the ventilator mask and so attempted to communicate through sign language. All I could get was, "I'm held." I finally gave up until we got home and that's when he emphatically wrote in huge letters, "I'm HEALED." I would not realize the significance of that declaration until later.

I went back into my training class and told the participants that our class would be rescheduled because I just got the news that my husband has moved to Heaven during the night. They looked at me a little strangely until the reality of what I said sank in. Every single one of them hugged me on their way out of the classroom and many told me they were praying for me. And here was yet another miracle.

I opened the car door and plopped down in the seat. I briefly put my head in my hands as I prayed for guidance and strength.

"Lord, I need you to help me get to my kids," I whispered through tears. I felt like I was a million miles away and didn't see how I could make it in time to get the airport at noon in order to get on the next flight home.

How do you get back up when it feels like the rug
has been pulled out from under you?

It was now 9 A.M. I was three hours away from the nearest airport and needed to get there by 12 noon in order to get on the next flight home. I also had to fill the rental car with gas, return it and get through security. I glanced down at my cell phone. The battery was super low, which meant that I needed to stay off the phone.

I also had to fill the rental car with gas, return it and get through security. I glanced down at my cell phone. The battery was super low, which meant that I needed to stay off the phone.

I can't believe I didn't go ahead and get a new phone
before coming on this trip!

I would normally have given myself a verbal lashing for my procrastination. I can sometimes be very hard on myself. I was tempted to go there but realized there were more important things to accomplish. I needed another miracle. I wished for the ability to 'teleport' myself.

At least I did something right last night. I unfolded the printout of the new directions that gave me a faster way to get to the airport. Little did I know how important this would be the next day… I was going to need all the help I could get.

It started sprinkling as I pulled on to the main highway. I turned on the radio for the first time since I had rented the car. I found another miracle because it was set to a Christian station. The very first song they played as I started my journey was: "Blessed Be the Name of the Lord."

159

Blessed be Your name—On the road marked with suffering

Though there's pain in the offering-—Blessed be Your name.

Every blessing You pour out—I'll turn back to praise.

When the darkness closes in, Lord, still I will say.

Blessed be the name of the Lord—Blessed be Your name.

You give and take away —My heart will choose to say—Lord, blessed by Your name.

As I started singing this familiar song it took on new meaning. It's easy to sing this song when all is well in your life and you're on the receiving end of blessings. Now I was on a new road marked with suffering and pain due to the death of my dear husband. He was the love of my life. He was the one who had learned, over the years, to finish my sentences and be my biggest cheerleader.

Even right now it comes down to my choice. I've always spoken of the power of my will and the choices I make. This somehow seemed different. But it wasn't. Here I was, speeding down the road to get to my family. It felt like I was a million miles away. I could choose bitterness or I could give all I was feeling to the One who would give me just what I needed.

When the darkness closed in, I had a choice to make right then. It is one I had made over and over during the hard times we had gone through with my husband's illness for the past decade. I could run from it, I could hide behind my anger and justify my resistance, OR I could choose to bless His name in this dark time. "My heart will choose to say…"

But Lord, I'm not ready yet.

Even as those words escaped my mouth, I knew it was an excuse. The mercy and grace showered on me during the difficult times we'd faced recently had all been preparing me for this morning, this minute and this second. As the chorus came around again I started to sing with all my might …

160

"You give and take away." I chose to bless the name of the Lord – even in this dark time.

The painful knot in my chest dissolved as I sang.

No matter how dark it seems right now the light of hope shines through.

At that precise second, I drove from the tree-lined highway to an open area where the sky seemed on fire with a beautiful heart-shaped cloud with a shaft of light shining through a hole in the middle of it. It felt like I was driving right through it. I smiled as I remembered all the times that these brilliant rays of light (or hope rays as I like to call them) had filled the sky just when I needed to be reminded of God's care for us. I smiled and felt the close presence of the Lord.

"I will trust You, Lord." At that moment I prayed a prayer of surrender and in response I received just what I needed to keep going. Just when we think we can't keep going we get just what we need in response to simple obedience. That's truly a miracle.

The next song that played on the radio was "I Can Only Imagine" where they sing about how we cannot even imagine what those who go before us see when they get to Heaven. For the next hour and a half it seemed like the entire play list had been selected specifically for me at that precise moment.

I made it on time for my flight home. It was a small jet that had a row of single seats on one side. I was assigned to the one in the very back. I put on my sunglasses and quietly cried the entire way. I saw the snapshot of the hope rays every time I closed my eyes. This is a journey that I didn't think I was ready to start. There are many changes and there is pain. Yet my heart will choose to say, "Blessed be the name of the Lord."

We never know what we're made of until we face a crisis. I don't think we're ever ready for "the call." How should you respond when you get the news of personal tragedy and loss of life? I don't think there is any specific "right way" to react. For me, it was like being kicked in the stomach. In fact, I had to run to the bathroom before going back in to the classroom to tell the participants we had to postpone their training. The rest of the day had a dream-like quality where events blurred, yet feelings remained strong.

This last year has been one of the hardest years of my life. I have continued to do each next thing I felt I needed to do. I have given myself permission to cry and truly feel the sorrow. I've also learned some very important lessons that I want to share with anyone who has experienced the death of a loved one.

1) You don't have to be strong. When I went back to finish the training session that was interrupted by "the call," many came up to me to tell me how much they admired my strength. I looked them straight in the eyes and said, "That was a supernatural strength that came from God." It felt like my weakest moment, yet a divine strength flowed through me as I did the next thing I needed to do.

2) You don't have to be in a hurry to "get over it." Grieving has no formula, no timetable, no agenda and no schedule. Take your time; relive the memories and enjoy the good times. Cry over what you've lost and mourn the anniversaries of events you would have shared. Pull out the pictures and embrace the pa Harrisville screwed up why home for those heading back to myin. Give yourself time to feel deeply. Through it all, invite the Presence of the one who can best comfort you. Ask Him to carry your sorrow.

3) You don't have to stop enjoying life. There is a reason you are still here. Find reasons to laugh. Enjoy those closest to you. This last summer I took my entire family to California to significant places that were important in my husband's life. It was a bit extravagant yet so rewarding. I was able to mourn another set of memories and chapters of our life together. We had so much fun as we spent time together and celebrated the life of a remarkable man. My grandsons enjoyed Disneyland, and learning how to surf.

We created a new set of memories that honored the legacy of their Papa—a generous man who loved them so much.

162

Keep looking for "hope rays." I look up on cloudy days. It's now a hope "habit" to search the clouds for the opening where that beam of light breaks through. It's catching on with others around me and they share their pictures with me. I challenge you today to look for miracles and expect them on a consistent basis.

Hope gives us the strength to celebrate on dark cloudy days,
knowing that the sun is still shining behind the dark clouds
even when we can't see it.
Just when we most need them, beautiful rays of sunlight can
break through the clouds touching our spirits when we were
about to give up and reminding us that there is always hope.
Therein lies the miracle!
~ Karen Sebastian

ᏩᏍᎤᏍᏎ

About the Author

Author, speaker, corporate trainer, ordained minister and Hope Catalyst, Karen Sebastian enjoys sharing her rich life experiences with others—engaging them in adventurous discoveries of the beauty of hope in a dark, cloudy world. Karen's personal journey from despair to hope followed many challenges: serious health issues, infertility, a prodigal daughter, caring for her disabled husband, and recently becoming a widow—all foundational in her heart place of writing "The Power of Hope for Prodigals: Prepare the Way Home," and most recently, contributing to *{An} Unsinkable Soul* anthology in order to further inspire hope. Today, Karen loves early morning walks, capturing photographic sunrise images, and creating a legacy of unforgettable memories for her beloved grandchildren, while living life full out in the spirit of hope! You can contact her at karen@karensebastian.com.

CHAPTER 19

Precious Stones

Lisa Smith

I have come to believe, through all that I have experienced and those whose paths I have crossed on my journey in this life, that every challenge that presents itself in the disguise of adversity can be dealt with in one of three ways: despair and victimhood; resistance and denial; or acceptance and action. The first leads to retreat, the second to limbo, and the third to progress, growth, and new possibilities.

❦

Precious stones can only be created under extreme pressure.

In 2006, my resiliency and "identity" was severely tested when in the span of three weeks I experienced four of the top major life stressors:

1) I was laid off right before Thanksgiving.

2) I became self-employed with my own business.

3) The love of my life broke up with me to be with another woman.

4) I turned 40—and my dreams of marriage and children seemed lost.

My sense of security, familiarity, and where my life was headed came crashing down.

It took all my internal and external resources
to not have a breakdown and climb into a valley
that would have been hard to get out of.

Yet by relying upon and continually reaching out to those resources I had been gathering all my life up to that point, I was able to keep pulling myself up out of the dark places my mind tried to take me, putting one foot in front of the other, and eventually recognize and become grateful for the growth these events allowed me to experience.

The first blow came when my boss called all six of the employees of our hypnosis center into his office for a "quick meeting" as I was preparing to have for the night. He shared that he had been losing money since taking it over the previous year and just couldn't keep it afloat anymore. Not only would he need to close the doors in just 10 days, he asked us not to tell the clients because of all the legal repercussions.

That was really a moral dilemma for me. I felt an obligation to my clients who had contracts and were expecting them to be fulfilled and get the help they had paid for. And I had developed trusting relationships with them as their hypnotist and coach. They were going to come back from Thanksgiving break and find the office closed with notification coming in the mail.

Yet, I also wanted to honor my boss's request to do it this way because he and his wife were really caring people and had been trying to save the business from a previous owner and manager who were driving it into the ground with the changes they were making. Plus, he had a plan to help alleviate the gravity of the situation, which involved me taking the clients into the part-time home-based hypnosis business he knew I had.

Although I worked full time for the hypnosis center, I also saw my own clients on occasion in my home office at night or on Saturdays. I only made a couple of hundred dollars a month—if that—and it was far from a serious business. Taking on the clients from the center would be a huge undertaking and require a lot of changes to how I had been doing things on my own. It would also require me to commit to doing it full time instead of trying to find a job doing something else.

This led to another dilemma and huge decision to be made. Could I really pull off this transition and support myself being self-employed? Did I have enough ability to run my own business and wear all the hats that required—seeing clients plus finding new ones, doing the sales process, running the administrative aspects, dealing with the finances, etc.

But if I didn't, what job options did I have? I had a bachelor's degree in marketing, but my marketing career had been abandoned when I started with the hypnosis center nearly eight years previous. I didn't know if I could even find a job quickly in marketing or what pay I would be able to get since my skills were outdated.

I felt like a rock in a hard place. And for a variety of reasons, I had to make a decision fast. I reflected on a deeper level and tapped into my long-time belief that "everything happens for a reason" and a quote I had stuck to my mirror for years since I first saw it:

> *The Universe is always conspiring in my favor;*
> *only good comes from each experience.*

I realized that I was being given the proverbial kick in the butt out of the nest so that I could find my wings and fly as a full-time hypnotherapist making a bigger impact in the world with my passion and my gift. I had been contemplating it for years yet was too afraid and unsure to make the move until this happened.

I then saw it as God's way of giving me another big sign, as She's done many times in my life, that I had to pay attention to and act upon to step onto my next path. And because it seemed to create a win-win-win scenario for all involved—the clients, my boss, and me I made the decision to take on the task and make the leap into full-time practice on my own.

I won't go into all the details of what it took to have the transition happen, but it was a very busy, stressful, overwhelming experience. Thankfully, there were enough clients who were willing to make the transition with me and whose payments I was able to take over and have sufficient revenue to maintain my current income level. This allowed me to work for "free" with clients who had already paid the Center in full so I could fulfill their contract time and keep them happy.

Once the decision was made, I had to inform all my friends and family. For some reason, I felt embarrassed about it along with being scared. I still remember how difficult it was to get the words out of my mouth past the tears and tightness in my chest. The support and hugs and assurance I received that my family and friends would be there for me, with whatever I needed, allowed me to feel a sense of relief and as if a weight was lifted. As did all the supportive and encouraging emails I received from other family and friends when I let them know.

Unfortunately, the next blow came when the support I thought I would also get from my five-year boyfriend—who I felt was the love of my life even though he didn't feel the same—was taken away when he told me just after Thanksgiving that he had met someone else that he wanted to start dating. Although I had broken up with him two years earlier (the hardest thing I've ever had to do) because he was clear that he didn't want to get married, we continued to be involved with each other since that time.

He had not dated anyone in that time but knew that I was actively dating people from time to time, though no one sparked my interest enough to become serious with. Alas, I was still comparing everyone to him and not able to find someone to help me move on no matter how hard I tried.

My biggest fear was realized when he told me that he had net someone new, would not be able to be my "date" at the 40th birthday party I was planning for myself, and requested that I come and get the rest of my various possessions from his house.

He was kind about it, but "ughh!" Talk about a knife in the heart! A tidal wave of thoughts and emotions hit me all at once and it was all I could do to not break down and start screaming and sobbing, while I tried not to let him hear the despair in my voice, remain mature and keep my pride intact as I calmly told him thank you for letting me know and I'd call him later to arrange a time to come get my things.

That was perhaps the longest day and night of my life. My sleep, which was already difficult because of the stress and concerns of getting my business going, was even worse. I cried and screamed at God, "Why is all this happening to me?" "How much more can I take?" "When will it get better?"

My pillow was stained with tears every night for a while. I could barely eat anything because my stomach was upset all the time, and I lost 12 pounds in 3 weeks. I was a mess. I finally broke down and bought a box of sleeping pills just to try to get some rest so I could wake up and get out of bed every day. Many mornings, upon opening my eyes, when I remembered what was happening in my life, I just wanted to stay in bed.

But there was a strength and resilience inside me that wouldn't let me. Having a purpose—my clients to see and help with their problems—is the main thing that kept me getting out of bed, showering and dressing, and keep being seen.

My 40th birthday was also looming, presenting another reminder that I was not married with kids, as I had envisioned myself being at age 40 when I was in my teens and twenties. It was something I had always wanted and now—turning 40 without those things—seemed like a dream I would have to give up. That, on top of everything else going on, seemed like a milestone of failure and disappointment to me.

How could I celebrate being 40, single,
childless, and unemployed?

It was two weeks after the center closed and one week after my boyfriend's call, when I was faced with another big decision— how to handle my impending 40th birthday and the party I had already begun planning before any of these unexpected events occurred.

This is where I finally had my turn-around and began to bounce back. I reminded myself of what I'd shared with hundreds of clients over the years—and even with friends who were going through their own crises. That it's not what life throws at you that determines your happiness or success. It's what you do with it. Lemons are not good or bad; when life hands you lemons, you can choose to suck on them and feel bitter, or you can add some sugar and water to make lemonade and enjoy it.

It's the power of choice. I could choose what meaning to give to all these events and how to respond to them. My feelings and actions are my choice. As I acknowledged this, I began to feel empowered again. And I made an important decision:

I decided to embrace the change, find what to be grateful for,
and make the theme of my 40th birthday "My Second Act."

Over the next few weeks, things started to feel better. The anxiety in my stomach began to subside and I was able to eat normally again. I also found a natural homeopathic remedy for "racing thoughts" at bedtime (Rescue Sleep), which worked even better than the sleeping pills. I began to listen to hypnosis audios to release stress and anxiety and to reinforce positive, optimistic thinking. I started a success journal to write down all the positive actions I took daily and the good things that were happening in my business and my life.

I listened to inspirational music like Jana Stanfield's "Let the Change Begin" album, which is still a favorite resource when I need to feel re-inspired. (Note: I highly recommend you check out her music videos on YouTube, especially "If I Were Brave.") I reread the supportive email from friends and family. I spent time with friends and having fun. Even though I was on a very strict budget, I found low or no-cost ways. I joined a small but highly supportive Mastermind group for coaches with weekly calls to help support each other with our businesses by giving feedback, ideas, and encouragement; they were an immensely valuable resource for me for years.

And my birthday party? I dressed up in a fancy red dress, had my girlfriend put together a picture montage of my whole 40 years of life, had a blank board for people to sing their well-wishes to me for "My Second Act," and put out business cards and brochures for my new business to announce my decision to start my own full time practice and ask for referrals. I had over 40 people there—some new friends, some long-time friends, some family, some clients, and even my (now ex) boyfriend for a brief time, plus his brother and aunt. Despite the uncertainty of what lie ahead, it was a fun night that I embraced with enthusiasm and a new attitude of positive expectancy and adventure for what I could make of the next 40.

A lot has happened since that time. Seven years have passed and my business is stronger now than ever. I have helped hundreds more people improve their lives through the work we've done together and have countless testimonials and thank you emails from them, and have been awarded a "Best of Virginia Beach" award for the past five years.

Two years ago I started another division of my business, Marketing, Mindset & Manifesting, which specializes in coaching other coaches, holistic practitioners, and service-based business owners on the practical as well as psychological and spiritual aspects of running a business so they can successfully take that leap into self-employment like I did.

Although I am still single and without children, I have dated several wonderful men in that time and become a child mentor through a local mentoring program. I'm no longer pining over the old boyfriend thanks to using various energy healers and the inner clearing techniques I use with my clients.

If you're reading this story and resonating with any of the situations or feelings within it, trust that there is hope for you to bounce back as well. Here are the four Lifesavers that helped me and that I share with my clients to help them:

ONE: Change your focus. What you focus on expands. Instead of focusing on what you don't have, focus on what you do have and be grateful. Instead of focusing on what's not working, focus on what is and put your energy there. Anything else is a waste.

TWO: Change your story. What "story" are you telling yourself—and others—about the situation? Does it uplift you or deflate you? Does it cause you to be destructive or "stuck" in time, or to move forward? What meaning are you giving to the situation? How can you choose to change the meaning and "author" a different story with the chance of a happy ending?

There's also a process I currently teach my clients that helps them dissolve stress and negative emotions within a couple of minutes or less. I learned it from one of my teachers, Morty Lefkoe, though I already knew how to do it intuitively.

1) Notice the negative emotional response you're having to an event.

2) Notice the meaning(s) you've given to that event that has produced those negative emotions.

3) Clearly distinguish between the event and the meaning(s) you've given it (event ≠ meaning).

4) Ask yourself what new meaning(s) you can give to that event that would be more positive or neutral (come up with at least two).

5) Notice if the negative emotion becomes positive or dissolves, if not, go back to step 3.

THREE: Create a supportive environment. Be mindful and purposeful with what you're putting in your head. Have as many positive, inspirational, uplifting, encouraging resources around you as possible... what you read, watch, listen to, engage in, and the people you spend time with all influence your focus, your perception, your stories, your feelings, and therefore your action

FOUR: Take purposeful action. Don't get stuck in idle. When you take action (with the proper mindset you'll get in numbers 1-3 above), you will move yourself out of the situation you're in right now more quickly. It also allows you to regain a sense of power because you're doing something. There may be some things you can't control, but there are always things you can.

Just focus on finding at least one thing and do that. Another step will appear after that—I promise. You don't have to know all the next steps—no one does. You can just take the next one that seems doable and trust that there will be another to follow. God has your back, just as She has always proven to have mine, even when things seemed hopeless.

I can honestly say now that despite what seemed like a really horrible time in my life seven years ago, I truly love, appreciate and am happy with the person those experiences gave me the opportunity to become and the life I am experiencing now. What will be the gift(s) in your challenge?

"Whatever good or bad fortune may come our way, we can always give it a meaning to transform it into something of value."
~Herman Hesse

ख़्ळ८०

About the Author

Lisa has owned and operated her own personal and professional development business, Life by Design, LLC, since 1998, taking it to a full-time practice in 2006. She holds a Bachelor of Arts degree from Westfield State University in Marketing and Communications, and is a Certified Mindset Coach, Master Hypnotherapist, EFT Level 1 and NLP Practitioner in the Virginia Beach area.

For more than 17 years Lisa has been professionally trained and active in the field of human performance coaching and transformation. For nearly eight years, she was employed as a HypnoNutrition Coach and trainer with the national hypnosis franchise, Positive Changes Hypnosis Centers.

As an avid writer and professional speaker, Lisa has written and published numerous articles locally and nationally, produced numerous hypnosis and mental conditioning audio CDs, and co-authored two additional books on self-improvement. A current Director of the Hampton Roads Public Speaker's Association, Lisa presents lively talks and workshops to teach people how to more effectively use and improve the mind to achieve personal and professional goals, and been interviewed on local and national radio stations.. She is also a Life Member of the Virginia Junior Chamber and a Senator for Junior Chamber International (a designation given to less than 1% of all Jaycees in the world).

Lisa can be contacted through her websites at www.mmmcoach.com and www.hypnocoachlisa.com .

CHAPTER 20

Waking up After Depression

Valerie Sorrentino

As Martha Graham said in my all-time favorite quotation, "There is a vitality, a life force, an energy, and a quickening that is translated through you into action; because there is only one of you in all of time, this expression is unique. And if you block it, it will never exist through any other medium and it will be lost. The world will not have it. It is not your business to determine how good it is nor how valuable nor how it compares with other expressions. It is your business to keep it yours clearly and directly, to keep the channel open. You do not even have to believe in yourself or your work. You have to keep yourself open and aware to the urges that motivate you. Keep the channel open."

ᎧᏒᏦᏩᏕᎧ

This is at the heart of my story; this is my mission as well.

It was a beautiful, effortless, serene and magically relieving moment. I remember the smile that I felt flowing through my whole being. I remember the lightness and the loving embrace I felt as I experienced freedom for the very first time. It was heaven. I felt the comfort and magical white plane of heaven and I thanked God be bringing me here.

It was bliss.

Until, I… woke… up! It was even more devastating than the day before when I was overwrought with dread. It had been a long road of despair during that year after I held my second child for the first time.

Having two children so close together was, let's just say, an adjustment. I soon found out sleep deprivation is a traumatic condition. My sad discovery that I was still among the living brought me to a depth of depression I didn't know possible. Actually, I wasn't even aware of the depression itself. Funny what denial hides from ourselves, yet shows to others around us.

So, let's dial it back and I'll tell you the whole story. I went from typically lost, fairy tale marriage and life with two beautiful babies. Bronze golden boy and lovely little baby girl—twenty months apart. Our business was growing in a quantum leap. We were enmeshed in a partnership with family. We all lived together while our new homes were being built. There was A LOT going on. I was hiding my ugliness as best I could but it came out in aches, pains and dissatisfaction.

I was handling it all with the skill of any brand new mom, wife and entrepreneur. I wore a happy face. After all, I had it all until one split second… then suddenly, without warning, my whole life changed. When I bent over to pick up the fluffy stuffed animal on my way to nurse my five-week old girl, I hit the floor with a crash. It was abrupt, it was excruciating and it was impossible to understand. Aren't we invincible as young adults? Aren't we able to do it all, be it all and have it all? Apparently not... I was pretty sure my body would be fine, but my bruised perception of no pain-no gain would kill me.

When I hit the floor with a slap, my husband ran to see what had happened. All I could say was, "Get the baby. Get the baby." I needed to nurse her. *How could I let her starve?* When we could get me to my feet because of the writhing pain, I begged him to bring her to me and slide her under my side. "Roll me onto her!" We got her to latch on and nurse while the tears rolled down my cheek to the cold tile floor.

When things were calmer, after the baby was fed, I got a lift to the recliner and parked there for days. Imagine the fear of hurting your infant from any kind of painkiller or muscle relaxer while being a nursing mom. Imagine the humility to be in the center of the living room as a young inexperienced mom in the middle of a busy family household. My face was green—that's what my mother-in-law told me.

My hair was dirty. My baby was helpless and my
toddler was on the loose.

Have you ever felt so helpless, weak and afraid? I didn't know I could be so fragile and incapable. I was only 26. After taking the meds (guilt), I felt more numb than relieved. I felt more sick than sedated. I felt like a spectacle and I could feel the control of motherhood slipping from my grasp. In the following months I would become "out of control."

What is a bulging disc anyway?
What is Prozac for? Why am I taking so many pills?

My identity had changed so much in the recent 24 months I couldn't even recognize who I was.

Who am I and why am I here?

179

And the questions grew into, "I'm so helpless why would anyone love me?" I still had the healthy drive and the duties of a new wife, but there was no way I felt remotely sexy or attractive that year and for years to come.

To make a long dramatic, slightly self-indulgent, story short, Let me cut to the time when I spiraled into the fit of rage and confusion—hitting my hands on my loving husband's chest crying, "I just can't take it! I can't take it **anymore!**" And I meant it. I felt the need to leave this earth... if you know what I mean.

It was the first time I said it. He looked at me and asked me, "What?? What can't you take?" He just didn't see it. He couldn't see the pain I was wading through. He didn't notice the sinkhole I had stepped into and was nearly over my head drowning in pain, inner torment and deep depression. I yelled out, "I'm DEPRESSED!"

Silence. We both were quiet as the truth lingered in the air of our brand new, freshly built home. We had beautiful sunlight shining in the west-facing window and the kids were napping peacefully. For some reason, I couldn't join into the ease of our life. For some reason I felt alone, afraid, confused and lost.

I got ready for work anyway and felt like a disappointment as I showed up with a slightly darkened smile. "I'll buy some makeup," I thought to myself. My face needed some help. It was time to conceal the dark circles and the pale lifeless complexion I couldn't bare to reveal.

Sometimes being a mom can be lonely. When you are in the house for hours at a time or racing home to keep up the night shift, you can find yourself letting go of friends and socializing that was a good part of your life only months before. Popping pain ills, anti-depressants and tranquilizers to get through the day was not part of the dream life. I had to make a change or life was going to make it for me.

The morning I dreamt of my blissful passing was one of the saddest days of my life, not because of an untimely passing, but because I woke up and realized the tormented life was still going on. It was my reality.

I wasn't handling it very well. I wasn't handling what life was giving me. I wasn't handling it well at all.

In the depth of my inner knowing—a place I was once very familiar with and comfortable in and a place I had abandoned in the tidal waves of change—I heard a voice with a revealing statement that led me to ask myself a life altering question. "We create our own reality." I knew this to be true in my core. It shook me there. I asked myself the question, "If we create our own reality, then why would I be creating this one?" This tortured reality was my own doing? I'm responsible for the pain, numbness, atrophy, nerve damage, sleeplessness, hormone upheaval, irrational fits, madness, yelling and screaming? Yes. I was. I came to know this and I decided to change.

It was a calm and conscious decision. It was a deep truth that I felt at ease with, but I had no skills in creating the woman I wanted to become or felt robbed of embodying. It would take time, training and lots of trial and error. It would take strength, support and a new level of honesty. It would take a miracle.

When I began to listen within I could hear my unhappiness so loud and clear. I listened more deeply inward and found a place of longing. It was only when I took action on the things I was longing for that I felt a sense of direction. It was when I got totally clear on what I REALLY wanted to say—without anger or guilt—that I found courage to be truthful. When I found the deeper truths that gave me courage to speak up, I undeniably became a stronger woman. But I had lost all my strength in the need to be strong; I was holding up under a façade. After choosing to put down the façade and face the life I was really choosing to live, I found a

181

drive and inner purpose and a momentum I never thought existed. I had a purpose.

Here's what I did and I ask you to consider a similar path when you begin anew.

1) Get clear about your true intentions for this life. Take the time to write it down. As if your life depends on it—get that clear and be that truthful with yourself.

2) Find a comfortable place to sit and dream the possibilities. Be sure to have a place of beauty to rest the eyes. In other words, create a lovely space for yourself.

3) Clear out old, stagnant stuff. This is a big one.

4) Enlist help. One person can't do it all alone.

5) Find a better conversation. Get involved in something you are genuinely interested in and then talk about it. Attract others that are attracted to your own interests.

6) Learn a positive language. A negative life is filled with negative words. Change them into positives and see what comes out of it.

7) Move your body. Often! Take up yoga and stick with it. Walk, run, swim, play a sport. Get the chemistry of feeling good to run through you.

8) Learn to relax. Practice often.

9) Commit to a gratitude journal until living gratefully is a way of life.

10) Always find the gift.

11) Find a healing modality that agrees with you. There are so many.

12) Meditation, EFT, Quantum Touch, Feng Shui, Reiki, The Work, massage, reflexology, acupuncture, and so many more. There is Mind and Body but also Energy Psychology. Explore the alternative world of healing.

13) Find a teacher, mentor, coach, classroom, library of new information that supports the positive life you are learning about. Become informed and supported.

182

14) Own your feelings. They are there for a reason. Notice if they are in balance or OUT of balance. Are your feelings all negative or all positive? A little of both?

15) Practice self-acceptance. Unconditional love. Start by practicing it on others.

16) Change your crowd. Let your environment be uplifting where ever you go. (Especially the environment between your ears)

17) Set appointments and then show up. Decide who you'd like to be and begin to show up that way. Healthy, energized and well rested?

18) Strong, fit and awake? If this isn't working out then discover what you don't like about where you are headed... make better appointments.

19) Empty your closets of old worn out stuff that isn't who you want to be.

20) Change your eating habits to a vegetable rich, sugar free, more natural source of foods.

21) Give yourself the gift of follow through. Keep doing what you are doing to get to know who you are at your core. The core values you care about, the ability to love and be loved unconditionally and stay involved in your own interests. Know that you matter.

Here is the big one—when I did this it changed everything for me and for my life with my family.

Drop the habit of complaining.
This will change the whole nature of how you deal with your feelings and the way you see people around you.
Replace the problem that comes up with a positive solution.

From the time I "decided" to change my reality, I began a journey of self-discovery. I found peace and pain relief in the practice of gentle yoga. It was combined with the knowledge of physical therapy and proper body mechanics. I never got back surgery and live pain free today. It has been part of my life's mission to teach others the same through restorative Hatha yoga teaching for 15 years.

It was my mission to create a home with a happy loving environment to grow in and be supported while being able to relax. I really put everything into a positive place for body, mind and harmony.

Through the study of environmental psychology and proper placement, Feng shui, dowsing, space clearing and EMF's, I help spiritually aware sensitive people create a positive place to live and thrive in.

In the study of the healing arts I have found great peace of mind and body while teaching my students the important skill of staying grounded, in retreats, group classes and virtual classes, as well.

Proper nutrition is a fundamental for well-being, good health and happiness. I help others clear out the toxins from their diet while staying at ease and relaxed. It can be stressful to learn new eating skills.

Meditation and yoga is a mainstay for a very happy and healthy mind and body. The inner wisdom of one's heart, soul and life purpose are revealed in the quiet of the peaceful practice. Life becomes art as we stay connected to one's central self. I found my mission is to help make the world a more beautiful place by teaching well-being and positive living choices through soft power.

I am absolutely thankful for the crash I had in my earlier life because it is that big of a contrast to the wrong direction I was heading. The pain was my big red indicator light that I had a malfunction in my system. It was the malfunction of paying attention. I now know that world peace is possible. At least, it is in my world.

I welcome you there. My gift to you is found at www.Valsgift.com . Join me in a virtual tele-series called Healthy on Purpose and apply for my course The Simple Art of Manifesting to get very clear on the direction you are headed. In short:

1) Become clear on your life's intentions

2) Be very grateful

3) Detox your mind and body regularly with yoga, meditation a clean eating

4) Detox your life and relationships by not complaining

5) Relax and love unconditionally

Namaste'

"There is a vitality, a life force, an energy, a quickening that is translated through you into action, and because there is only one of you in all of time, this expression is unique… Keep the channel open."
~ Martha Graham

෬෫෭ක

About the Author

In the quest for personal development and self-discovery, each person has defining moments in life. As the go-to person for personal development in a gentle, graceful and effortless way using the power of crystal clarity and the courage of personal truth, Valerie Sorrentino guides them to break the chains of expectation and experience the power of personal truth. An author, healer, spiritual entrepreneur, transformational teacher and speaker, Valerie rebuilt herself from the inside out—emerging as a lover of inner wisdom, gentle kindness and truth in her transformational processes. This world class transformational teacher and expert stress relief specialist, happy to be contacted at Valerie@LifeEnergyCoach.com, resides in San Diego,

California, sharing her personal philosophy, "Often, it's not about becoming a new person, but becoming the person you were always meant to be, already are and are dying to express."

CHAPTER 21

Life as I Know it...

Anna Weber

I am not sure I will ever understand why we are frequently so reticent to be grateful for every beautiful, blessed thing that comes into our lives. No! It is more a basic human frailty that we take our dreams and aspirations and "expect" certain things to materialize in ways that align with our expectations! It is often only when we get the "goodies" we desire that we openly express our gratitude.

ೞഔഔ

When life takes another direction, it can be a difficult shift to make, when *Life as we know it...* ceases to exist. It calls for courage and conviction and a desire so strong we draw on the capacity to embrace a new "*Life as I know it!*"

Life as we know it... is filled with lessons we simply must learn along the way – some more bittersweet than others and some we find ourselves repeating and wondering why that is so. The following were my own life lessons – all recurring themes about a world that doesn't protect children, a world, where in my own heighten expectation of being taken care of was never to be my reality, and a world where it took me far too long to exercise self-love and self-care. Perhaps, had I been more astute earlier in life, I would have learned these lessons without ever having to repeat the learning process – perhaps my story can get you "on track" sooner, rather than later.

Lesson Number One: Life is mercurial; it flows in beautiful, magical ways that we don't understand. Even in the things we find hurtful and ugly... if we remain open and receptive to that flow, in wisdom we can see how one door opens, allowing us to pass through on our journey, following yet another perfect path.

Lesson Number Two: We are not on this life journey by ourselves; there are many people whose lives we touch, knowingly or not. Sometimes we are in their lives so they can give to us; sometimes to teach us valuable, life-altering lessons; and sometimes, perhaps to be inspired by us. Many of our hurtful experiences teach not only us, but also those with whom we share them.

Lesson Number Three: Never make an agreement with yourself to "stuff" things into your attic world so you don't have to deal with them; they will only come out to interrupt your life at the most inopportune times and in the most inconvenient ways. Deal with life – face on! Agree, instead to manage self-care: emotionally, physically, mentally and financially.

Lesson Number Four: Learn to love yourself first! Learn to understand who you are and what you are made of. Learn the gifts life has given you and the skills life's opportunities helped you develop. Then embrace life's challenges and be in a place of gratitude that even though others in life may be there for you – you can still make a life for yourself and by yourself! You can have a life rich in give-and-take, with others who do love and support you —a life void of those who would in any manner seek to harm you.

Lesson Number Five: Until you learn to step beyond the hurts of the past and shift out of the attic world where you stuff all those painful thoughts and beliefs, and until you can learn that you are enough, that the world is enough… the easy things for which you can be blessed and for which you can be grateful, simply will not transpire in your life.

From what experience do I speak, that I earned the privilege to cite these five wisdoms to you? A seeming eternity of learning to shift my understanding of *Life as I knew it…* adapting, embracing change, and trying to be grateful in the face of life not being all I thought it to be! Let me share some of those with you.

My natural father passed away when I was but 18 months old; my stepfather came along probably by age three. An abusive, shiftless uncaring man, he created in me a cautious, conservative, but personally responsible being. *Life as I knew it…* called for my being always protective of children being abused, always adapting to new environments, new schools, new friends, and always carrying this underlying depth of anger and animosity at an adult world that would not protect its children.

Life as I knew it… changed more significantly at age 11 when my stepfather's abuse escalated from physical to sexual. In my quiet, take charge and take responsibility for my life attitude, I attempted to run away from home—grateful for finding the protective care of my loving, understanding older siblings for the next three years. My stepfather ultimately deserted my mom and younger sister so I returned home to what I expected to be a protective, loving, maternal environment. Although financially life was difficult, I was daily grateful there was some normalcy day to day. I excelled in school, had the fortune of bonding with life-long friends, and although my mother's work required her spend most of her time in a near-by town to work, and left my younger sister in my care, I knew what to expect each day and adapted accordingly.

I have grown to believe it folly to expect life to be all we "think it should be!" There are reasons for changes, whether we understand them or not, and changes will always happen. *Life as I knew it…* took yet another turn the summer before my senior year.

189

My mother shared that she could no longer take care of me – felt that I was not able to take care of myself – and that she was encouraging me to marry someone who would take care of that for me! Broken in spirit and low in self-confidence, and questioning once more why the world is not a place that protects its young, I agreed to the marriage – providing I would in no way be prohibited from graduating! After all, I had been in honor society since I was in junior high, was very grateful for the talents and skills I had to share with others, and felt passionately it would almost be a sin to "settle" for giving less than my all in life; academics were the golden star to which I so tenaciously held.

Fast forward—some four years and *Life as I knew it...* threw me for another loop! My husband turned out to have sexual preferences alien to me, and our differences escalated to one moment of physical abuse to which I was not willing to have repeated. Grateful that I had been given a beautiful, intelligent and loving son, I once again made an agreement with myself to adapt, realizing my place was to protect, nurture and care for him. Consciously, with strong will and deep determination, I set aside my constant under-current of wondering about a world where no one was up to seeing to my well-being. I moved forward – grateful that I had the strength, skills and desire to move ahead with my life and do right by my son.

Another man entered my world... a man with a desire to succeed that matched my own; a man that appeared loving and able to help me create the best world for my son. I was more than blessed to have two more children from this union. However, the emotional connection and strength of being loved was quickly distilled when shortly after my beautiful daughter's birth he communicated, "I think we made a mistake, I don't think I really love you." *Life as I knew it...* took another path on my twisting journey!

Committed to not disrupt the lives of my now three children, I was determined to stay in the relationship regardless the cost to myself. Little did I understand one of life's realities is that if you don't exercise self-care, be it physical, mental, financial, or emotional – the well will soon dry up and all those subconscious demons you try to keep locked away bubble their way to the surface to disrupt your life, your health, your happiness.

A divorce ensued after close to 15 years – a process that left me absolutely reeling! *How could the man I married even be remotely connected to the person I experienced during our divorce proceedings?* Determined and directed, I continued to believe in myself, and my intention to provide the most positive environment possible for my children. After all – they did not deserve to be in a world where adults didn't care for the needs of the little ones. In retrospect, in reacting to certain negative events during that period of time, I may not have made all the best possible decisions on their behalf, but it was not for a lack of thinking I was.

A few years later I entertained the idea, once more, of sharing my life with someone else whom I felt could provide balance and stability in my life. Married in mid-January, by Valentine's Day he had decided he was still in love with his former spouse, but we both subsequently determined to make a go if it. *Life as I knew it...* for the next eight years became a struggle with his infidelity, controlling nature and subsequently positioning me to walk out the door with nothing but my clothes, books and music! I was just grateful I had been able to participate at a high level with my son and his children, be more supportive of my daughter's needs, earn my Master's Degree, and able to purchase a little home where I felt I could settle down for the balance of my life.

I was then able to assist my daughter for a couple of years while her family built their dream home, build my coaching practice and thought that *Life as I knew it...* was finally on the way to being on track! I had finally come to understand that I didn't need someone else to take care of me or be responsible for me. God had given me infinite skills, talent and passion – enough to fill every need or desire I held or could dream of! To this day, I am most grateful – not only for that freeing recognition, but the reality that it is so!

In 2009, I discovered my daughter was in an abusive relationship; imagine my emotional turmoil that I was so blinded by thinking she had a life for which she should be grateful that I was not fully emotionally present to recognize her situation or protect her! The past few years included a focus on helping her and her two beautiful children to survive and learn to thrive again – not wanting their lives to share my scars of feeling the world is a place that does not protect children! Some days I want to scream, "Suffer not the little children!" but I wonder… who would hear me?

Unfortunately, during this time, my physical body said, "Enough!" It finally responded to my years of stuffing feelings down deep, demanding too much of myself emotionally and physically, and not exercising self-care. *Life as I knew it…* was now a relationship with a rather rare form of mammary cancer and an introduction to holistic healing! Cancer was perhaps the greatest gift in my life! I caught a lot of flak from family and friends that I was reticent to share my situation with them. I simply did not want it to define who I was, nor did I want someone telling me how to deal with it! I had been fortunate to have friends and clients who experienced and believed in holistic healing and chose that as my path. Four years later… I am grateful for the results of those choices.

Today, *Life as I know it…* includes what will always be a continuing journey of self-care – a foundation that includes mental, spiritual, emotional and physical healing. I found that cancer took charge in my body; most likely a result of harboring so many negative feelings, pushing myself emotionally and physically beyond what is healthy, and always "stuffing" down that little girl pain of never being loved enough for someone to care for me and about me – always that prevailing belief the world was a place that does not care for its children.

Today, *Life as I know it…* includes a man who adores me, shares my spiritual journey, protects me, and will do anything in support of our collective children. I believe he is now in my life because I finally realized I didn't "need" to be taken care of by anyone – I can be filled with gratitude on a daily basis that I receive his love as a blessing. It is like he is the ice cream on top of the chocolate cake I will always be able to bake for myself!

The life with which I am blessed today reminds me to always exist in a continual state of gratitude for things big and small and to know that if there is a little "blip" in my expectations being aligned with my reality – time will reveal that I will have been blessed by that twist in life's path. I encourage you to look at your own life journey, find all that for which you can be grateful, and agree to open up and release those painful, debilitating thoughts you have allowed your subconscious to harbor for far too long. In that release, I trust implicitly that you too, have voices to put in print; lessons of wisdom to share.

"There's no scarcity of opportunity to make a
living at what you love.
There is only a scarcity of resolve to make it happen."
~Wayne W. Dyer

ଔଃଔଃ

About the Author

Anna Weber is a Literary Strategist who knows the value of sharing life stories in the quest of bringing wisdom and positive value to readers and guides sassy Entrepreneurs and savvy Service Professionals through the oft-time confusing and overwhelming journey of becoming successfully published. Anna, the CEO of Successfully Published, Voices In Print and Get Your Book Noticed, understands the realities of publishing, writing and marketing a book; having provided support to Debut Authors for close to two decades in an industry rift with constant changes and transformation. Anna, who also finds happiness in life traveling with her husband, and engaging in other creative ventures, can be reached at AnnaWeber@VoicesInPrint.com or

http://www.voicesinprint.com

CHAPTER 22

When Spirit Says GO...
You Listen

Ashley Welton

I didn't know what would come of it, but I knew I had to get out.

Six years in Los Angeles is a long time for an island girl. Having built my chops as a graphic designer, yet never quite seeing the success I desired, I didn't know where to go. I didn't know how to 'make it' in the wildly free, happy, and abundant way I imagined. So when my final employer / employee relationship concluded in October of 2009, the locks that bound me to that city unclicked one by one.

ೞಶಲೞ

New ideas were born and plans made. March would mark the beginning of a three-month South American sojourn. How was I to know that a three-month journey would morph into a three-year assembly of the life I yearned to live?

Had I known what was to come, I'd like to think I would say, "Heck yeah, I'd still go," but three years is a long time to stretch. In the scheme of living, three years is a pimple on a pubescent forehead, but these particular years consisted of a contortionist's aim for flexibility, a war widow's fortitude, and a boxer's persistence.

The biggest lesson imparted from that sojourn?
Listen and leap—you can thrive through anything.

Let's head back to February of 2010, and a day when I had a definite plan.

That plan was to convene with my friend and her boyfriend the day I landed in Lima, Peru. They'd travel up from Chile, I'd meet them, we'd surf, and eventually meander our way across the border, returning to Chile. I'd stay with them for a month and then, once South America and I had developed a deep and lasting love, venture out on my own. That was the plan, a soft landing of sorts.

Four days before my scheduled departure, God laughed at my plan. The sixth largest earthquake ever to be recorded by a seismograph, an 8.8, hammered the central Chilean coast. My friends lived at the epicenter; luckily they'd left for Santiago just hours before the quake hit. Two days passed before I could get ahold of them and comprehend the gravity of the situation.

They were okay, but nobody was going in or out of Chile for quite some time, and the surrounding villages lay in devastation. Tsunamis often do far more damage than a simple earth shake. They weren't coming to Peru.

I was on my own.

I could have stayed. But for years I wanted to shatter the shackles Los Angeles held around me. Everything was ready. Staying would hurt more than going ever could.

My mother, world traveler and all, gently suggested, "You could postpone."

"No, mom. I really can't." An urge roared forth from my deepest gut, "I *have* to go."

Sometimes you just *have* to go. Silencing a calling that Spirit dictates often causes more pain than stretching to answer it ever would.

I couldn't stay.

A 5 A.M. arrival in Lima, not a very safe or pretty city, necessitated making a reservation at a hostel with airport pick-up. A ride from the airport, and one night's lodging constituted the entirety of my new plan.

The morning of my scheduled deviation from a predictable life, my parents drove me to the airport. Three months fit into one backpack and a small shoulder bag. As I walked into the terminal, an unshakable fear clutched at me. I cried my way to South America.

When undergoing personal earthquakes, it's important to recognize the advocates around you. My parents are phenomenal people. They couldn't have stopped me from going, but they could have made it more difficult. Yet they watched their daughter struggle through fear and, instead of adding their own alarm, supported her through it.

They believed in my listening, they always have, and for that I will be forever grateful. Pay attention to your patrons, they'll shore you up when you think horizontal and immobile is your only exit.

I think my desperate fear stemmed from the fact that, in my subterranean self, I knew this journey was more than a vacation; it was a rite of passage from which I would not return the same. The apprehension grew from not knowing who that would be.

Upon arrival, however, survival and intrigue won the battle. With dry eyes, alert senses, and a keen openness, I met my driver, Miguel. He stood awaiting me outside the grimy baggage claim; sign in hand. I'd always wanted to be one of those people, welcomed to their destination by a waving sign and a smiling stranger. Wish granted.

On the drive, the Peruvian coastline grew into view, nestled between a rising sun and our halting conversation in broken Spanish. An hour later, we arrived at the hostel. Hostels are like petri dishes for forming new friendships. After sleeping off some jetlag, I joined the party and fit right in. On day three, I felt it was time to move, but I didn't have a plan and was afraid to go.

Luckily the angels were with me. They took the form of two South African ladies who had been traveling around South America on a tight budget for eight months.

In the courtyard of the hostel one of the angels asked me, "What are your plans?"

"Um, well, I don't have any." I admitted.

"Do you want to come with us?" she asked.

Desperate for guidance, I said, "Sure, when are you leaving?"

"In 30 minutes," she replied.

"Okay, I'll be ready."

And off we went. For two weeks I traveled with these ladies, learning the dos and don'ts of bus travel, food consumption, lodging location, and budgeting. Sweet inspiration on a wing, did we have some adventures! We sand boarded Oasis dunes, visited a Peruvian winery, floated in saline saturated waters, trekked to the second deepest canyon in the world, and fell in love with an old couple at their kitchen table. Ironically, I spoke the most Spanish of us all.

Eventually we parted, and I was on my own, this time only slightly afraid. Enamored with the Argentine bus system (it's far better than Peru's) I journeyed to Bariloche, the gateway of Patagonia, and promptly fell in love. Yes, you can absolutely fall in love with a place.

Bariloche is otherworldly. Draped in lakes and punctuated by mountains, the landscape grabbed hold of my heart the first morning I spent dreamily sipping tea and gazing over the lake. I said, to quite a few people, "I want to live here. I am going to live here."

The whisperings of spirit said, "You just may!"

I stayed in Bariloche for a couple weeks, exploring and allowing it to root deeply in the crevices of my heart, but after a time the need to continue pressed on my heart. This journey was intended for movement, not to freeze at the first site of love. "It's early," I told myself, "if after two months you're still in love, you can move."

Amongst all my adventures, I began to write. Every experience stimulated my desire to bring others along with me by uniting my words with their imaginations. When I wrote, the fire hot twinkle of life shot through me, and people noticed. Their reactions were unanimous, "Ashley, you're a writer!"

Writing was the first milestone to discovering my purpose positioned on a baseline of joy. The baseline of joy, however, wouldn't congeal until much later.

For two months more I adventured, explored, and looped the southern continent. Lust and loss and the transient nature of life presented itself, full frontal.

By the end it was decided – Bariloche would be my new home. A conversation in Cusco introduced me to an American in Bariloche who turned out to be the linchpin in my whole expat operation. Returning home as scheduled, I worked to drum up some cash, transferred the lease on my apartment, and packed up my life. Intending to stay anywhere from six months to a year, I fattened a snowboard bag, a backpack, and a computer bag with my belongings.

Once again my plan was prenatal. I had no friends, no job, and no house, just an address of the place I would stay for a couple nights, which turned into two weeks.

Amazing experiences transpire when you're open and roll with the boils. I lived in three houses; only the last one had my name on the lease. I managed to wrangle employment with an American snowboarding adventure camp doing graphic design and branding —big image stuff. I LOVED it.

That season however, like everything, had its end. The owners returned to America, and instead of moving with them to their New Hampshire headquarters as was offered, intended, and expected, everything fell apart and I was lost in Bariloche, scared, alone, and unsure of what to do.

> *Adrift again; this time I'm adrift in a foreign country where living is not easy, and jobs for outsiders are hard to come by.*

Working for the adventure company lit a fire in me. Staying in Argentina simply to play at discovery didn't hold the same enchantment. I knew what I wanted to do and was ready to move forward, but with my previous plan disintegrated, the "how" proved elusive.

With no money, and no options I turned to my genetic scaffolding. "Mom," I asked through tears one day, "can I come home for a while and figure this shit out?"

"Of course you can," she said.

What I imagined would be a six-month figuring transmuted into a two-year self-excavation.

Having left home at 15, and never wanting to live in Hawaii again, not once did I imagine myself at 28 at home living with my parents. It's the best thing that could have happened.

The year I stayed with them wasn't painful. In fact, it was an amazing opportunity to connect with my parents on an adult level, as friends. I surfed a lot, I wrote, and everything was good, except for one small hiccup—I wasn't making any money. Yes, I managed to get published in magazines and had stories running every month, but editorial doesn't pay much, and something about it missed the mark.

That year in Hawaii, however, yielded the second milestone to discovering my purpose positioned on a baseline of joy—the where. I knew, bones deep and to everyone's surprise, I wanted to live in Hawaii.

I had the what, writing.

I had the where, Hawaii.

But I was still sorely missing the how.

After a life of about-faces, I slung myself into another opportunity, investing $36,000 into real estate investment education courses, tore myself away from Hawaii, and moved to Long Beach, California where I would learn from those who had already succeeded in the business. I would use real estate as a means to support my writing habit (I laugh at that now) and vowed that I would not return to Hawaii until I could afford to live on my own without getting a second job and had paid off my education debt.

Now, that is a proper challenge!

South America was fun. It was an adventure. Yes, it was a stretch of faith, and had I not gone through it I wouldn't possess the diamond solid belief in myself that I could do anything, but this segment… it was excruciating personal growth, business education, real estate training, loneliness, and extreme wanting.

Starting a business and being an entrepreneur are like enrolling in a personal development boot camp. Nothing will excel or sink you faster. In fact, being an entrepreneur is straight up hard. The world isn't set up for entrepreneurs. So you'd better love what you're doing enough to pour every last drop of yourself into it, or it's not going to work—a lesson I learned the hard way.

My faith stretched like taffy on a wrapping machine. During this period, however, I developed friendships with people living lifestyles I wanted, and learned not necessarily how they did it externally, but how they did it *internally*. This segment of my life introduced me to the teachings of Abraham-Hicks, Napoleon Hill, Jim Rohn, and so on.

> It introduced to me the concept that you can have it all and it won't always be hard.

> It instilled in me the knowledge that the only infallible remedy for loneliness is to fall deeply in love with your own company.

> It showed me that I truly *can* do anything.

But it didn't make me money. I was putting in long hours, hard work, and lots of effort for little reward. There was no logical reason why the business wasn't working, and yet it wasn't, and I was miserable.

Then, at a seminar, I showed a friend some marketing material I'd written. His business was marketing, and being impressed, he suggested we work together.

Flattered, I declined the offer because I'd made a commitment to real estate. Writing would have to wait. Sometimes you lose sight of why you started; clearly I had.

Three months later, after *losing* money on a horrific deal, and making zero progress, I opened myself back to the possibility of writing. In the three months following that decision, I brought in more money writing copy than I had the previous year in real estate. When you're living your purpose, the money always comes.

For a while I tried to do both when I realized I was wasting time, and my misery persisted. From then on my sole focus was to build the foundation of my copywriting business, sell my two investments in California, and move to Hawaii—nothing else existed. Four months later, I was on a plane home.

Originally, moving home not only required that I could support myself, but also that my education debt had been paid off. There are times to compromise your intentions; May 2013 was one of them. So once again, I listened and leapt. Although it nearly broke me in the process, that year and a half tempered me. The three-year duration set me up to thrive.

Within one month of moving, I found my perfect residence. Within two months of moving, I met my great love. Within three months, I quadrupled my previous year's earnings. After searching, stretching, and at times writhing in desperate struggle, the synchronicity of those events shocked me. I spent much of that summer pinching myself at regular intervals to be sure it wasn't a dream.

Edgar Lee Masters said, "It takes life to love life." He's right, but falling in love with a life of your choosing requires avid listening, the courage to take chances, and the persistence to move forward even when you can't see the physical manifestation of your desires. Today, when my faith is stretched and circumstances don't appear to align with my aspirations, I remind myself, "Ashley, everything is always working out. Whether you struggle through or enjoy the journey is entirely your choosing, but know that everything is always working out."

No matter how many "Are you kidding me?" moments life throws in your path, everything is always working out for you, too. Those three years could have been easier, and perhaps faster, had I known that. But I don't regret one single moment I spent learning, growing, and developing a skill set that will serve me for my duration.

In those three years I discovered I can endure—and what's better—thrive through anything. It is that endurance and consistent pursuit of being a better, happier, and more giving human that built the foundation of joy that I now stand upon.

See, life will always deliver the unexpected; sometimes it's pleasant and sometimes it's stretch-worthy, but whatever you're dealt… know that it's temporary. If you focus all your energy with the single intention of finding joy regardless of circumstance, the hues of life will be brighter.

There is nothing you cannot be, do, or have when you listen, leap, and walk steadily forward, rooted in faith and poised on a baseline of joy.

"Everything is alright forever and forever and forever."
~ Jack Kerouac, The Dharma Bums

ଔଌଔ

About the Author

Sought-after copywriter, Ashley Welton, is an expert storyteller who uses her mastery of words to encourage others to do more, be more, learn more, love more, and LIVE MORE! The founder of Miniskirt Ninja Media, Ashley, who hails from Hawaii, breathes life into businesses worldwide—drawing on her uncanny ability to take risks that pan out. She thoroughly believes in making quantum leaps, the power of saying yes, and doesn't hold on to a lot, but drags her favorite books with her everywhere she goes. When she's not having an intimate dinner with her thesaurus, Ashley lives an enthusiasm-laced lifestyle and dedicates much of her time to surfing, traveling, exploring, and the general outdoors; connect with her at www.ashleywelton.com.

www.ingramcontent.com/pod-product-compliance
Lightning Source LLC
LaVergne TN
LVHW051507080426
835509LV00017B/1963